Launch your Recruiting Career

No Experience Needed to Get Started

By: Jonathan Kidder

Table of Contents

Chapter 1: Enneagram Personality & Strengths Finder Assessment	5
Chapter 2: How to Set Attainable SMART Goals	18
Chapter 3: What is a Recruiter?	23
Chapter 4: Understanding the Full-Cycle Process	36
Chapter 5: Understanding in-house / agency recruiting	49
Chapter 6: Setting Up Informational Calls with Recruiters	56
Chapter 7: How to Network for Recruiter Job Openings	65
Chapter 8: How to Land an Entry Recruiter Role with No Experience	77
Chapter 9: How to Ramp Up Your Recruiting Career	85
Chapter 10: Conducting an Intake Meeting	93
Chapter 11: Talent Sourcing & Searching	102
Chapter 12: Writing Job Descriptions and Posting	110
Chapter 13: Social Media, Recruitment Marketing, & Employment Branding	121
Chapter 14: Time Management Tips	128
Chapter 15: How to Phone Screen Candidates	134
Chapter 16: How to Produce a Talent Pipeline	151
Chapter 17: How to Submit Candidates	155
Chapter 18: Candidate Experience	162
Conclusion	169

This book was written to help professionals enter the recruiting industry with no prior experience.

Have you ever wondered how to become a professional Recruiter but didn't know where to get started?

Well, then this book is for you! I wanted to create a launch pad for professionals who are interested in changing careers. The world of recruiting is constantly changing and requires on-the-job training. You can become a Recruiter and be successful without having any previous experience or background.

Whether you are a recent grad or someone looking to change career paths altogether, anyone can learn to become a Recruiter without having attended a college or university degree program. Many top performing Recruiters make over $100,000+ per year — and it all starts with getting that first recruiting role.

I'm a seasoned Recruiter with over a decade of experience and have worked in many different industries and organizations. First, I will help you see if you would be a good match to become a Recruiter. Then, I will help you learn the fundamentals in recruiting and what you will need to know to be successful in your first role.

Ultimately, I hope the book will help you prepare for and land your first recruiting role. This book may very well change your life and I'm hopeful that it does.

<u>Who should read this book:</u>
- Professionals looking for advice on landing an entry level Recruiter position.
- Professionals who are looking to understand recruiting and talent sourcing fundamentals.

<u>In How to Become a Technical Recruiter, you'll learn how to:</u>
- Setting clear and attainable goals.
- Understand what a Recruiter does every day.
- Find and network for Recruiter job openings.
- Gain confidence with talent sourcing and conducting phone screens.
- Have a clear ramp up guide for becoming a professional Recruiter.

Chapter 1: Enneagram Personality & StrengthsFinder Assessment

The first question that you might ask yourself is: <u>Would I even be a good fit to become a Recruiter?</u>

I recommend taking a personality test to figure out your communication style and complete a strengths assessment to understand your top strengths and qualities.

The Enneagram personality model is used to understand someone's unique personality type. The origins of this assessment have been disputed but the main ideas started in the early 1950's. Enneagram is based on 9 different personality profiles.

Why would you need to assess and score someone's personality, you may ask?

- Have you ever wondered why people do things differently?
- Why do some people react differently to the same scenario?
- Maybe you want to understand how to communicate or work better with others?

- You wanted to understand your specific personality in a professional setting.

The truth is, we all have different personalities and unique qualities that play out during our daily work routines. The Enneagram model has been around for a while, but most recently, it has been trending. HR departments recognize the benefits of this test and have used it in addition to job description requirements, developmental team building exercises, and improvements for leadership management.

What is Enneagram?

Enneagram is a straightforward and direct way to understand someone else's personality based on 9 different profiles, which I've included below. I'm sure you will come to realize many of these personalities fit well within a Recruiter's personality and professional role.

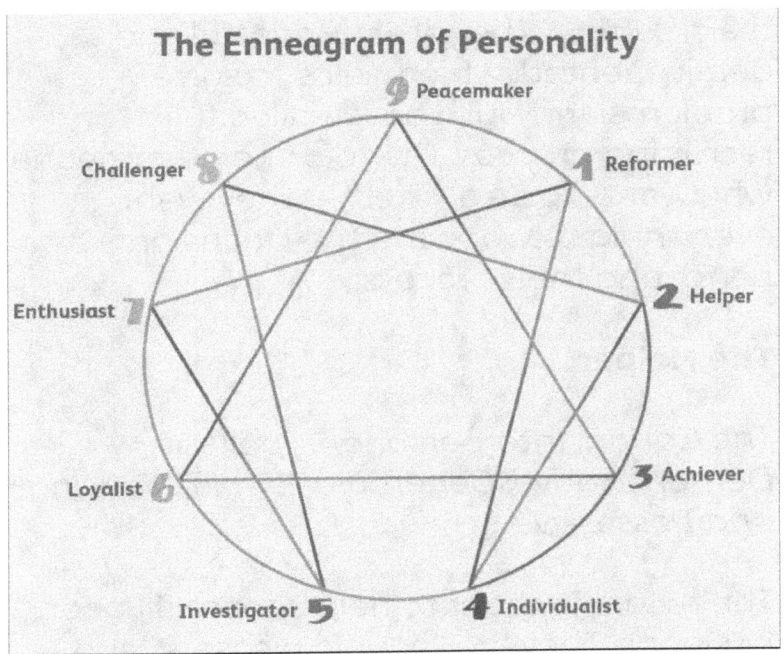

Here's the Enneagram Personality of a Recruiter. The views expressed are based on my own interpretation of each personality trait.

The Reformer

The Rational, Idealistic Type: Principled, Purposeful, Self-Controlled, and Perfectionistic.

The reformer fits well within the recruiting realm. They exemplify self-control, high standards, and help deliver results within a team setting. They are purposeful and detail oriented, which helps to solve problems and build a well-oiled full recruiting process. The reformer is someone who wants to be a "fixer" — they want everything to work and they focus on perfecting their process.

The Helper

The Caring, Interpersonal Type: Demonstrative, Generous, People-Pleasing, and Possessive.

The helper is eager to help a team fill open positions. They are "people pleasers" and want coworkers to like them. They want to demonstrate value and are good at directing others towards a certain team achievement. They are someone who loves connecting and building long term relationships. They value relationships with both candidates and coworkers and are always available to help. They are great team members to have on your side and always go out of their way to make others feel cared for. This might come in handy within the candidate experience parts of recruiting, as you will need to be supportive and foster a good experience throughout the process with your candidates.

The Achiever

The Success-Oriented, Pragmatic Type: Adaptive, Excelling, Driven, and Image-Conscious.

I am going to go out on a limb here and say that there are probably quite a few Recruiters out there who are achievers (myself included). The achiever is driven in their pursuit of results. They love to focus on projects and accomplishing daily goals. Achievers aim to impress, and they often deliver. This personality fits well into a sales or recruitment role as they are naturally highly motivated. This type also needs to be careful not to burn out in their pursuit of achievement.

The Individualist

The Sensitive, Withdrawn Type: Expressive, Dramatic, Self-Absorbed, and Temperamental.

The individualist values individual connections with others and is focused on authenticity and meaning. They want to know that their work has direct benefit in the lives of others and can use this motivation to meet recruiting goals. They value their uniqueness and benefit from their contributions being acknowledged. They may struggle with more monotonous parts of recruiting and need to work to find their own sense of meaning from what they do professionally.

The Investigator

The Intense, Cerebral Type: Perceptive, Innovative, Secretive, and Isolated. Investigators excel at critical thinking and research. They are highly intelligent and bring their immense knowledge and expertise to their job. This personality would fit well in a Lead Generation or Talent Sourcing role. They benefit from being given some space and independence and may need to work on being a part of a team, as this may not come naturally. When they have the skills needed to work well within a team, they will bring valuable strategic thinking.

The Loyalist

The Committed, Security-Oriented Type: Engaging, Responsible, Anxious, and Suspicious.

The loyalist is someone who prioritizes safety and structure. Once these are in place, they are extremely dependable and will help build a solid team and a smooth candidate experience. This personality type often anticipates problems and find solutions, which is a much-needed aspect of recruiting. This personality may also do well in a Human Services role that is based on helping to create safety and structure for others.

The Enthusiast

The Busy, Fun-Loving Type: Spontaneous, Versatile, Distractible, and Scattered.

The enthusiast is another common personality in the recruiting world. Enthusiasts are eager to jump on a new project but might struggle to finish it. When focused, they are able to be solution-oriented and turn problems into opportunities. They are sometimes unorganized and can be easily distracted, however, they showcase optimism and have a positive attitude within a team setting.

The Challenger

The Powerful, Dominating Type: Self-Confident, Decisive, Willful, and Confrontational.

I could see the challenger being a good fit within a recruiting manager title. Being self-confident and able to share feedback is important as a recruiting manager. This person is good at delegating and directing others within a team. They may dominate team meetings and may sometimes get confrontational with others. This can be positive if the challenger frames their confrontations with others in a helpful way. As long as they temper their forcefulness, when necessary, challengers can be great leaders.

The Peacemaker

The Easygoing, Self-Effacing Type: Receptive, Reassuring, Agreeable, and Complacent.

This type might be best suited for a Human Resource Generalist role. Peacemakers are kind and agreeable. They value routine and process and have a balanced approach to work. They are often able to see multiple sides of an issue which can greatly benefit a team's perspective. At times, they may struggle to stand up for themselves. When functioning well, peacemakers bring a sense of calm collectiveness to a team.

I strongly recommend that you take the Enneagram assessment. This is a great way to understand how you work in a team setting professionally and outside of work. It will also help you understand if you are suited to become a Recruiter.

What is the StrengthsFinder Assessment?

To become a Recruiter, it is important to understand your key strengths.

The Clifton StrengthsFinder assessment was created under the leadership of educational psychologist Donald Clifton. He wanted to identify the skills of the best of the best to capitalize on them.

The Clifton StrengthsFinder is an assessment of "normal personality from the perspective of Positive Psychology." When you purchase a code, it grants you access to take the online assessment.

How the online assessment works:

177 pairs of "potential" self-descriptors are listed in the assessment.

The descriptors are placed as if they are anchoring polar ends of a continuum. You choose the descriptor that best describes you, and the extent to which it describes your personality.
After 20 seconds, the assessment moves onto the next item pair. If you miss too many questions, the assessment will start over.

Once you've completed the Clifton StrengthsFinder, you'll immediately receive the results – it will rank your top 5 signature themes in ranked order. Your individual results will also include a packet of information specifically geared to your unique skillsets.

In a culture that focuses on developing or fixing our weaknesses, the StrengthsFinder tool invites us to focus on what is already positive and strong about us. Knowing your top strengths will make you a better Recruiter.

Below are the 34 strengths that the assessment will rank you on:

STRATEGIC THINKING

Analytical
Context
Futuristic
Ideation
Input
Intellection
Learner
Strategic

RELATIONSHIP BUILDING

Adaptability
Connectedness
Developer
Empathy
Harmony
Includer
Individualization
Positivity
Relator

INFLUENCING

Activator
Command
Communication
Competition
Maximizer
Self-Assurance

Significance
Woo

EXECUTING

Achiever
Arranger
Belief
Consistency
Deliberative
Discipline
Focus
Responsibility
Restorative

Once you've determined your major strengths, it's time to look a little deeper into each one to understand what they mean for your personal and professional career. Are you someone who prioritizes discipline and can't rest comfortably at night with tasks left unfinished? Or, perhaps, someone who values communication and can easily network a room filled with strangers?

After you've spent some time reflecting, it's time to show off what you bring to the table to the rest of the world. I recommended including your top 5 skills on your LinkedIn profile and resume to enhance your summary and highlight some of the things that make you great.

Of course, these steps are something aspiring employees in *any* field should take, but it's especially important to complete the assessment if you're considering following the recruiting path. First and foremost, it will reveal whether your personality and communication skills are a right fit for the career, saving you countless hours if you realize your efforts are better suited elsewhere.

And, since you'll be responsible for finding candidates and evaluating whether their strengths fit the role needing to be filled, it will only make your job easier. By having already undergone this process yourself, you'll recognize which workers have a clear understanding of their personal strong suits — and which ones need more time to figure it out.

Chapter 2: How to Set Attainable SMART Goals

Every achievement starts with a clear plan and attainable goals. If you want to become a professional Recruiter, you will need to know how to build a plan, as the profession needs someone who can stick to daily routines and set long term goals.

Goal setting is something everyone is familiar with. However, knowing how to set realistic ones and create a strategy for achieving them is essential when it comes to being a successful Recruiter.

Goals serve as a sort of road map for us, marking a clear target and providing a step-by-step process that helps us stay focused as we make progress and try to get from point A to B within a specific time frame.

All too often, people set goals that are too vague or too far out of reach. However, by understanding the SMART goal process, the likelihood of achieving your recruiting goals increases significantly.

What are SMART goals?

SMART, which is an acronym that stands for Specific, Measurable, Attainable, Realistic, and Timely, is a great way to help you stay on task and maintain motivation to meet multiple deadlines so common in the recruiting industry.

When creating each SMART goal, identify the following details:

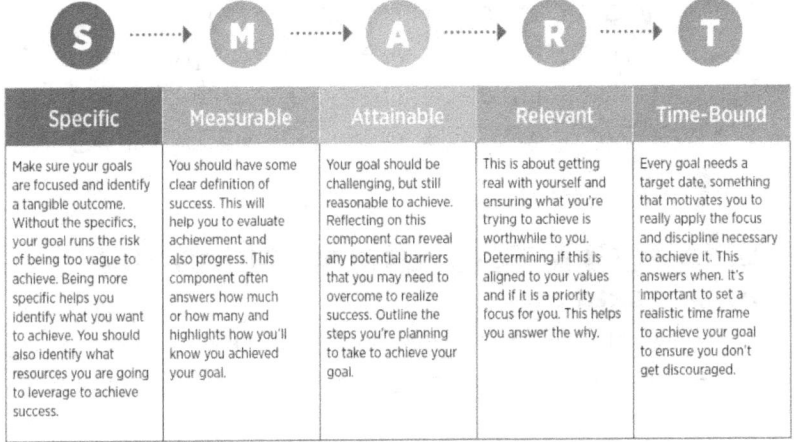

Specific	Measurable	Attainable	Relevant	Time-Bound
Make sure your goals are focused and identify a tangible outcome. Without the specifics, your goal runs the risk of being too vague to achieve. Being more specific helps you identify what you want to achieve. You should also identify what resources you are going to leverage to achieve success.	You should have some clear definition of success. This will help you to evaluate achievement and also progress. This component often answers how much or how many and highlights how you'll know you achieved your goal.	Your goal should be challenging, but still reasonable to achieve. Reflecting on this component can reveal any potential barriers that you may need to overcome to realize success. Outline the steps you're planning to take to achieve your goal.	This is about getting real with yourself and ensuring what you're trying to achieve is worthwhile to you. Determining if this is aligned to your values and if it is a priority focus for you. This helps you answer the why.	Every goal needs a target date, something that motivates you to really apply the focus and discipline necessary to achieve it. This answers when. It's important to set a realistic time frame to achieve your goal to ensure you don't get discouraged.

Source: Capd.mit.edu

Specific

Be specific about the goal you're setting. As a Recruiter, you're often helping to fill a position, but it's important to focus on the smaller details. For instance, understanding the specifics of the position for which you're hiring will enable you to effectively use your time and resources. Additionally, meeting with the hiring manager helps you learn what skills, talents, experience, and education will be required of the individual. So, try to set a realistic goal, such as improving your monthly hire goals, time to fill, diversity hires, quality of hire, and candidate surveys.

Your goals can first reflect your job searching efforts as well. Maybe you want to spend an hour each day networking, set up an interview once a week, or something else.

SMART Goal Suggestions during your initial search:
- Applying for job openings.
- Networking outreach with Recruiters online.
- Setting up informational calls.
- Number of Recruiter interviews.

Measurable

With the details above, you'll be able to create job descriptions and marketing campaigns that target the right type of client base. Additionally, the criteria will enable you to track and evaluate applicants and hire quality candidates faster. This type of data not only helps you make necessary adjustments but will also motivate you by displaying a physical representation of your progress.

Achievable

You should always set goals that help you serve clients as quickly and efficiently as possible. However, it's important to make personal goals, too.
Create milestones that will motivate you to improve as a Recruiter. For example, how many more job placements do you want to make this year, versus last? One study reported that 56% of Recruiters make at least 11 placements each year — consider setting that as your main priority.

Reasonable

A goal should always be attainable, rather than being so far out of reach that you simply give up out of frustration. Ask yourself: Do you believe the goal and the allotted time frame are reasonable? Do you have the necessary resources available? Does the goal resonate with you on a personal level? Are you committed to making it happen?

Time

A goal without a timeline is no different than a casual thought or suggestion. So, set a beginning and end date for your goals for a sense of urgency. Otherwise, it will fall by the wayside.

Start making achievements

Setting SMART goals will help you improve your recruiting processes with clients and can also help you excel on a personal level. The bottom line: You can use the SMART goal method in your daily recruiting efforts or during your initial job search.

Chapter 3: What is a Recruiter?

Now, we've spent some time reviewing the backbone that'll support your efforts towards becoming a Recruiter. You know how to evaluate yourself and understand what strengths make you a good fit for the position, as well as how to create goals that'll keep your professional life moving at a rapid pace.

But with all this in mind, there's a question you still might not know the answer to: Do you know what being a Recruiter truly is?

If you're reading this book, you likely already have a vague answer in your head. Maybe you've seen the role portrayed in your favorite television show, had a family member recommend the career, or simply saw an advertisement online.

Regardless of how clear (or unclear) your perception of the recruitment profession might be, it's always a good idea to go over the definition and expectations that come with the title. Who knows: Reviewing the job in-depth might make you realize it's not quite what you thought it to be — or, hopefully, simply reignites your passion for the profession.

What does a Recruiter do?

Even if you've only been in the job market for a short period of time, you've probably crossed paths with a Recruiter or two already. For many industries, they are a crucial component that keeps organizations running as efficiently and smoothly as possible.

After all, a business is only as good as the employees it can get on board, which is why Recruiters are always on a constant search for the best candidates they can find to fill their empty roles.

Still, the responsibilities of a Recruiter can extend far past a simple job interview. The core fundamentals of this position (discussed in-depth in Chapter 3) include:

Managing staffing needs

As a Recruiter, a major aspect of your job will be spent *preparing* for recruitment. This means working closely with your hiring managers to understand which positions need to be filled, how many, how soon, and what kind of candidate should take the spot. By determining these factors beforehand, you'll hyper-focus your efforts on the things that truly matter and increase your success rate in the process.

Forming recruitment strategies

Another part of recruitment preparation has to do with your overall strategy. With so many new methods available to reach out to new candidates, it might be tempting to try each one at random to see what works. Unfortunately, this will only waste time in the long run.

So, to prevent wasting their energy, every Recruiter dedicates some time towards creating their hiring strategy. They may place an emphasis on digital recruitment solutions like LinkedIn, attend hiring events to meet applicants in-person, ask for referrals from other businesses, or adopt a hybrid approach.

It might take you a while to understand what works for you and what doesn't, but once you've identified the tools and methods that land the best results, your recruitment tasks will be a breeze.

Of course, networking is one of the main areas to focus on while developing a strategy. Industry relationships are like bridges, expanding your reach and unlocking an entirely new area filled with potential candidates. Some common networking methods include:

Attending job fairs and hiring events
Reaching out through social media
Joining public or private networking events
Prospecting out cold outreach methods

Reviewing candidates

This recruitment task isn't known to be particularly easy, though it's one of the most crucial aspects of the entire process. Once a Recruiter has thoroughly reviewed the company's staffing needs and outlined a strategy to follow, they can finally begin sourcing candidates they'd like to consider for the position.

This is also the part that separates a good Recruiter from a bad one. Effective Recruiters will have spent enough time on the previous two steps to know where to direct their efforts and how to use them to achieve success. They'll know how to separate relevant candidates from incompatible ones and set reasonable expectations. At this point, some general tasks also come into play, such as performing background and reference checks.

Overseeing interviews

Perhaps the most well-known part of being a Recruiter, the interview process is when all this preparation slowly begins to reveal results.

By now, the Recruiter will have sourced, reviewed, and narrowed down the list of candidates to those who are most likely to be a good fit for the position. Now, they'll need to coordinate interview times, inform candidates about what they should expect, and follow-up with those who are invited to the next stage of the hiring process.

A Recruiter might also be responsible for performing interviews themselves as a "pre-screening" to determine whether they should move on and speak with the hiring manager. Fortunately, these are often done over phone or video call rather than in-person, though that makes it no less important.

Following up

A Recruiter's job isn't quite done the moment they hand over a candidate to their hiring manager.

Even if most of their focus is spent on the points listed above, a part of the process also involves overseeing elements of post-placement once a candidate has settled into the position. This means checking in with the candidate to identify any issues they're experiencing, speaking to the hiring manager about their feedback, and coming up with solutions for any road bumps that appear along the way.

How much do Recruiters make?

Knowing what the role will expect of you is one of the first things to understand before you start your journey, but it usually goes together with another common question: How much will you make as a Recruiter?

As with most careers, the answer can vary. Still, there are a few general salary norms you can expect to encounter depending on your career path.

For starters, we'll need to discuss the two different types of Recruiters in the business: internal and external. Though their duties remain largely the same, payment standards differ between the two. So, which one will make you the most money?

External (Agency) Recruiter salary

These Recruiters work for a staffing firm/agency, which other businesses can outsource to help them find candidates for their open positions.

Now, what makes this position interesting is the way external Recruiters are paid. Rather than provide a flat salary, most staffing firms pay their employees through commissions. Now, this is where things can get slightly complex, since it's all based on percentages.

Here is how the process usually works out:

The company outsourcing the staffing firm typically agrees to pay them 15-20% of the candidate's starting base salary once the position is filled. So, if the job's first-year compensation is $100,000, the staffing firm could earn up to $20,000.

The staffing firm assigns a Recruiter to fill the position, who will receive up to half of that amount as payment.

If all goes well and the position is filled, the staffing firm holds $10,000 and pays the Recruiter $10,000 in commission.

As you can see, this means an external Recruiter's salary depends largely on their performance. The faster they fill a position (with a quality candidate, of course), the more money they will make.

So, those first starting out shouldn't expect to immediately rake in six figures. Still, it's worth practicing your skills, as more experienced Recruiters can take home upwards of $200,000 yearly.

Internal (In-house) Recruiter salary

On the opposite end, a Recruiter might opt to work for a company's internal HR department. This means they'll be solely sourcing candidates for *one* business, rather than for multiple clients.

Though these are probably the most widely available positions, they also offer some of the lowest salary options for those hoping to enter the recruiting field. Since internal Recruiters are paid salary instead of commission, their earnings may be limited to as low as $35,000. Those who spend a few years in the field can expect to earn a higher wage through promotions, though it's difficult to achieve a six-figure salary as an internal Recruiter.

Alternatively, a short-term contracted in-house Recruiter usually makes more, though their highest earnings stop at around $104,000 annually based on indeed averages.

Those who spend a few years in the field can expect to earn a higher wage through promotions. Many recruiters make over $100K+ after 3-4 years within the field.

Here's a break down of a Talent Acquisition teams roles:

Recruiting Coordinators

Primary Responsibilities:

- Primary point of contact to schedule phone screen and onsite interview.

- Sends invites to both candidate and interviewers.
- Finding interviewers to participate in Loops.
- Sends light prep information to candidate including presentation information.
- Sends scheduling information on detailed prep session (with Client Lead) to candidates.
- Assists in administering any tracking documents that help with scheduling initiatives like interviewer lists or interview structure.

Tasks they aren't responsible for:

- Recruiting activities related to bringing in new candidates into the funnel.
- Managing the process itself, as in changing or amending process. They are facilitators of the process set forth by Recruiting/Business Leaders.
- Changing interviewer list or anything related to the interviewer roster. They execute on the roster they are given.
- Sourcers

Sourcing Recruiters

Primary Responsibilities:

- Responsible for driving initial sourcing efforts to put candidates into top of funnel.
- Works directly with Hiring Managers in their assigned area to build pipeline.
- Conducting intake call with Hiring team for area to gather position requirements (if needed).
- Initial outreach to candidate using all sourcing resources available.
- Conducting initial phone screen with the candidate to determine base skill levels, fit for role etc.
- Pushing candidate into phone screen stage if they meet criteria.
- If not inclined at phone screen stage, calling candidate to reject.
- If inclined at phone screen stage, pushing candidate into the final round stage
- Managing phone screen interviewer roster and onsite interviewer roster based on area or hiring manager.

Tasks they aren't responsible for:

- Rescheduling interviews or sending invites to candidates/Hiring Managers.

Full-cycle Recruiter / Client Leads

Primary Responsibilities:

- Content approver of new reqs created within area.
- Providing general leadership of sourcing strategy to drive more results.
- Preparing candidates for onsite interview with prep calls, either group or individual.
- Attending all debrief sessions within your area they support to be recruiting point of contact for hiring decision.
- If not inclined at on site interview stage, calling candidate to reject.
- If inclined at on site interview stage, driver of offer negotiation, working directly with Hiring Manager as partnership to secure offer acceptance. This includes outreach to candidate to explain compensation program, benefit questions, and any other questions candidate may have.
- Primary point of contact for submitting offer exception requests if offer exceeds compensation levels.

- Primary driver of providing data reporting and data analysis of each area. Sending out weekly or bi-weekly report summaries to business.
- Responsible for running each Recruiting Progress call with business to review data, progress and action items.
- Responsible for general interviewer calibration monitoring, partner with business to ensure interview construction meets quality criteria.
- Managing phone screen interviewer roster and onsite interviewer roster based on area or hiring manager.

Chapter 4: Understanding the Full-Cycle Process

Still positive recruiting is the right career for you? Great!

Now, let's talk about some of the methods modern Recruiters utilize daily to power their efforts: In this case, the full cycle process.

Sometimes referred to as end-to-end recruiting or full life cycle recruiting, this approach sees Recruiters involved in every step of a comprehensive recruitment process containing six different stages (which we'll get to soon).

Still, your interactions with the method might look different depending on your employer. Since it's such a holistic undertaking that requires a significant time investment, some HR departments might have one specialist dedicated to each step of the process. Alternatively, they could have a full cycle Recruiter oversee the entire process — something more common in smaller organizations.

So, what is full cycle recruiting and — most importantly — how might you utilize it throughout your future recruitment efforts to source the best candidates possible? Let's take a deeper look to find out.

The Full Cycle recruiting Process

As I mentioned above, full cycle recruiting involves six steps that are crucial to follow. Even if just one is missed, the entire process could go off the rails — so don't forget them!

Preparation

You already found out the role preparation plays in Chapter 2, but it's worth emphasizing again, especially when it comes to full cycle recruiting.

This stage begins immediately once the job requisition (i.e., the request to create and fill a new position in the company) is approved. Following this, the Recruiter will schedule an appointment with the hiring manager (known as a vacancy intake/intake meeting) to understand what type of candidate they're seeking.

Requirements a Recruiter should gather information about includes:

Behavioral Based Personality traits:
- Work skills
- Experience
- Capabilities
- And more!

To make this smoother, a Recruiter can also come prepared to showcase their hiring data and talent mapping strategy, which will help them identify high-potential candidates with qualifications that align with the manager's priorities. They should also come prepared to discuss overall sourcing strategies and diversity hiring D&I goals.

After the vacancy intake, the Recruiter should have everything they need to write an accurate, comprehensive job description — one for internal purposes and another for external job postings.

Candidate sourcing

After meeting with the hiring manager and conducting an intake meeting. The next phase for the Recruiter involves candidate sourcing. This is where you start using their sourcing skills to identify potential candidates to fill the role. If they're looking to close a highly specialized position, this step might take more expertise to find potential leads. I've written a book titled: *Talent Sourced* that covers more in-depth talent sourcing strategies.

The sourcing channels they use to discover applicants can vary, though a few popular options include job fairs, hiring events, messaging candidates on platforms like LinkedIn, and in-person networking.

Online searches also remain a tried-and-true method. But, with so many profiles and documents cluttering the web, most Recruiters rely on Boolean strings to bypass irrelevant results. They'll follow something like the template below:

intitle:resume OR inurl:resume OR intitle:bio OR inurl:bio

A good Recruiter will likely use a mixture of different approaches to spread their net wide and simultaneously collect several "backup" candidates for future roles.

Of course, communication with the hiring manager doesn't stop here, as the Recruiter will be responsible for telling them about their progress and, if necessary, receiving updates regarding their requirements.

Candidate screening

If the Recruiter's sourcing efforts go well, they'll have connected with potential candidates and can begin reviewing them to judge their compatibility with the company and its open position.

Now, this *isn't* where the interviews happen. Since there are often many candidates, Recruiters need to "pre-screen" each person to reduce the group to solely those with the most promise (usually no more than 10 applicants).

<u>There are a few options Recruiters can use during this step, which include:</u>

Resume review:

Anyone who's applied for a job in the 21st century knows the role AI resume software plays in the hiring process — and this is something you could be using as a Recruiter yourself. There are dozens of time-saving tools available to help Recruiters determine which resumes are worth their time, and which ones aren't quite ready for the position. They can also involve the hiring manager on selecting and reviewing resumes if more vetting is needed.

Phone call:

Typically performed after a resume review (or immediately, depending on their process), Recruiters will call a candidate to discuss the position. They'll go over potential deal-breakers like work hours, expectations of the role, compensation, benefits, and other topics to ensure it's a good fit.

Pre-selection tests:

As one of the more advanced options, Recruiters can also turn to pre-employment assessment software. These solutions are incredibly comprehensive, putting candidates through personality tests, virtual job previews, cognitive testing, and much more. As such, they're usually used by major companies dealing with a high volume of applicants.

Candidate selection

The Recruiter's hard work has paid off, and they've now narrowed down a group of great candidates. Still, the process is not quite over.

Though it might not sound all that impressive, the Recruiter will now focus most of their attention on scheduling. Candidate interviews will need to be arranged, re-arranged, canceled, and — finally — performed. Some Recruiters will even have candidates go through multiple interview rounds, each led by a different team member, before being pushed to a final round.

During these efforts, the Recruiter will still work closely with the hiring manager to discuss which candidates made the shortlist, which ones seem to be the most qualified, which ones fell short of expectations, and more.

Still, despite the extended period it might take, all this effort ensures the Recruiter is as prepared as possible for the next step.

Candidate hiring

Following one or several rounds of interviewing, the Recruiter and hiring manager should be left with one to three potential candidates. Now, it's time to do even *more* deeper into each applicant to see which one is the best fit.
To do this, Recruiters will:

Check their references to confirm their skills and gather additional information.
Perform a background check.
"Rate" candidate data to see which one ranks highest according to the position's predetermined criteria. After the final round, usually the hiring team will discuss the candidates interview and decide on if they would like to proceed with an offer.

At the end of these steps, the Recruiter should have a clear idea of who should take the role. After discussing with the finance and HR department for approval, they'll reach out to the candidate with the offer — as well as inform those who didn't make the cut.

Employee onboarding

Good news: The bulk of the hard work is now over!

If the offer was accepted, a qualified candidate has successfully undergone the hiring process and become an employee, keeping the business powering forward with another capable worker at its side. However, the Recruiter can't sit back and relax quite yet.

As excited as they might be, new hires always need to be carefully guided into their position. So, during the "pre-boarding" period (which occurs after they've signed the contract, up until their starting date), the Recruiter will remain in contact.

Depending on the Recruiter's involvement with the company, as well as the company's own hiring practices, there is a diverse range of methods they might use to keep the new hire from feeling overwhelmed. They might invite them to a casual meeting to discuss any initial worries, share additional information about what to expect, connect them with members of the team they'll be joining, and more.

Don't worry; Recruiters aren't attached to their candidates forever. Following their first day, the company's HR team will be responsible for walking them through their employee onboarding program. However, they should still make themselves available for the occasional question or concern during those first few weeks.

***

Now that you know its basic structure, it's also essential to know *why* the full cycle process is such a staple amongst the industry. For a clearer picture of its role, I've listed some of its main advantages *and* disadvantages below.

Advantages of the Full Cycle Process

Enhances candidate experience

No company wants to put their applicants through a difficult time during the hiring process. Unfortunately, this is usually the case for those who oversee hiring without a solid outline, especially if they're a smaller organization or a major corporation stretched thin.

The full cycle process helps avoid this problem. Since hiring managers and Recruiters have a clear step-by-step plan to follow, they know exactly what to do and when to do it. Furthermore, they'll be able to grant each applicant an equal experience that places everyone on a balanced playing field, allowing them to create meaningful relationships in the process.

Reduces time requirement

Though companies *should* be willing to invest time into their hiring efforts, it's equally important for them to create a process that is as time efficient as possible.

While it isn't immune to the occasional roadblock, the full cycle process grants a Recruiter greater control over the time it takes between receiving an application and onboarding the candidate. Since the method relies heavily on efficient organization, there's reduced room for errors and a larger focus on accurate, relevant metrics. Furthermore, it ensures the same person (or people) oversee the entire process, eliminating delays caused by changing roles.

Improves candidate quality

The quality of a company's candidates might seem arbitrary at first glance, but the *way* they choose to collect them can have a significant impact on how good their applicants are.

For starters, we've already established the improvements the full cycle process grants on the Recruiter's side. They'll be more organized, focused, and eager to discover individuals who fit the role best.

As a result, applicants who aren't quite ready are automatically eliminated from consideration thanks to the pre-screening step, leaving behind only the most qualified, highly skilled candidates.

Disadvantages of the Full Cycle Process

Requires advanced skills and experience

Recruiters fresh to the field are rarely given the task to oversee the full cycle process alone, simply due to the extensive number of skills required to handle each step.

In some cases, companies and staffing agencies form an entire team dedicated to the process — something a smaller organization might not have the resources to accomplish.

Can lead to high workloads

As you've probably realized, the full cycle process requires a *lot* of time and attention from the Recruiter. Because of this, those faced with a high number of applicants — such as for a general role within a major company — might not have the capacity to go through each step without becoming overwhelmed.

The Takeaway

The full cycle process is an incredibly powerful tool Recruiters have been using for years. When it works, it allows them to hyper-focus their efforts and provide companies with highly qualified candidates in half the time.

Chapter 5: Working as an in-house Recruiter vs. agency-based Recruiter

Earlier, I briefly went over some of the options you have when it comes to choosing a Recruiter role and — more importantly — the salary expectations that come with them. Chances are, you still haven't made up your mind. After all, it's quite an important decision.

The good news is that, for now, recruitment isn't going anywhere. Companies always require hiring professionals to help them foster workforces capable of handling modern requirements, so there's little reason to worry about job prospects flatlining anytime soon.

With that being said, you now know that the *type* of job prospects out there aren't all identical. So, let's investigate these paths a bit more, reviewing the aspects that make them unique.

Working as an in-house Recruiter

Also known as an internal Recruiter, these roles are held within a single company. As such, in-house Recruiters will usually deal with the same hiring managers regularly and solely look for candidates for that business — no one else.

Responsibilities

Since they're only filling roles for one company, in-house Recruiters are usually able to focus on a relatively unchanging set of requirements. Along with the standard hiring steps found in the full cycle process, they'll also place extra emphasis on how well a candidate aligns with the business's culture — something they'll have a better understanding of thanks to their position within its workforce. And, since in-house Recruiters primarily look to fill permanent roles, employee retention will be at the forefront of their efforts.

Required skills

Paired with exemplary communication skills and an encouraging personality, in-house Recruiters tend to lean towards the "people" aspect of the hiring process. At its core, their purpose is to provide the company with only the best of candidates they know will uphold its mission.

As a result, they'll need to be well-versed in the art of employee retention. That means knowing how to solve problems quickly and amicably, maintaining steady communication with colleagues, knowing how to work well with others, and being able to discern the top choices from a pile of applicants.

Salary

In-house Recruiters are paid salary rather than commission, as an agency-based Recruiter would. In the United States, the average base pay for the role sits around $56,000 per year (Indeed). Of course, one can expect salary increases with promotions, though even the compensation for a senior position could be less than what an agency Recruiter makes.

Working as an agency-based Recruiter

Sometimes as an external Recruiter, these roles are held *outside* of a company's standard HR team. Instead, agency Recruiters work with a staffing agency and are paid through commissions, often focusing on filling short-term and temporary roles. As such, they typically work with a higher volume of applicants for a range of different industries and companies.

Responsibilities

An agency Recruiter is primarily focused on sourcing applicants quickly, though without sacrificing the quality of candidates. Most organizations rely on an external Recruiter to fill their temporary and short-term roles, which means there's little to no emphasis on candidates' cultural fit.

Required skills

In some ways, you could compare agency Recruiters to salespeople. Their success is based on how effectively they can "close" on a candidate in the shortest period possible, so that they can move on to the next position that needs to be filled.

Because of the fast-paced nature of an agency Recruiter, they must be very careful not to allow lesser-quality candidates slip through the cracks. So, if you're debating this option, ensure you can work well under pressure without taking a hit to your efficacy.

Salary

Some staffing agencies offer their Recruiters a base salary, but their primary earnings depend on the commissions received from each role filled. As a result, the most competitive and effective agency Recruiters enjoy salaries much higher than their in-house counterparts, with some achieving up to $200,000 yearly.

Working for yourself

That's right: There is a third option!

To put it simply, becoming a freelance Recruiter isn't the easiest. Though it closely mirrors the skills and responsibilities of an agency-based Recruiter, this career path depends largely on the relationships and connections you have at your disposal. Since recruitment is such a crucial aspect of modern business, most companies won't be keen on hiring a freelancer without references and a proven track record of success. As such, most Recruiters wait until *after* they've spent a few years working as an in-house or agency Recruiter before breaking off on their own.

Still, if you're able to do it successfully, you'll enjoy the freedom of choosing who you want to work with, when you want to work with them.

Getting paid as a freelance Recruiter is also a bit more flexible, since you'll set your own rates. A common strategy is to charge 15% of the yearly salary of the role being filled as the placement fee. Like an agency Recruiter, this means your earnings rely on the number of candidates you can source within a year.

The Bottom Line

Deciding what type of recruiting career to pursue isn't an easy task, but by looking closely at each route and comparing it to your personal skills and expectations, the road should be a little clearer.

Here are some key takeaways to think about moving forward:

In-house Recruiters

Great for those passionate about the "people" side of recruitment. Lower pay, but less intense and more specialized.

Agency-based Recruiter

Perfect for the competitive go-getter who doesn't mind a fast-paced workload. This can result in high pay, though experience is needed to achieve the largest earnings.

Freelance Recruiter: An alternative for those who'd rather work for themselves. Offers maximum career flexibility, though it can be difficult to get your foot in the door.

Don't worry if you're caught up in trying to make a choice — there's still plenty of time to figure it out.

Chapter 6: Setting up Informational Calls with Recruiters

Chances are, you're still pondering what recruitment path would be the best for you and your goals. With so many different factors to think about, from salaries to experience level, it all might seem like an impossible puzzle to solve.

There's no reason to worry; you don't need to figure it out alone.

Before we move onto other aspects of the industry, you should think about what questions you might want to ask a Recruiter if given the chance. Is there a certain concern you can't find an answer to on your own? A piece of information you want to confirm?

Well, you won't have to wonder for very long.

In this chapter, I'm going to tell you how to set up an informational call with an active Recruiter to learn everything you want to know. In fact, most Recruiters are happy to talk about their experience and give advice to someone else considering the practice — after all, they've been in your shoes at one point!

What is an informational call?

Like the name suggests, informational calls are *informal* interviews with someone who works in your area of interest. As such, neither party should approach it as if it's a formal meeting: the interviewer isn't (and shouldn't be) asking for a job position, and the interviewer isn't considering them as a candidate. Although it can serve as a networking opportunity, that's not the primary purpose of the call.

So, in that case, what *is* it supposed to be?

Well, it's better to think of it as a casual conversation. Since you're not being judged as an applicant, you can feel free to ask everything sitting in your mind regarding the profession. Furthermore, the person you're speaking to will feel more relaxed and willing to answer your questions, which might cover topics such as:

- Different career paths within the area (even those you didn't know about).

- The "ugly truth" behind the position.
- What it's like to work for a specific company.
- Insider tips and advice for how to secure a role.
- People you should try networking with to increase your chances of receiving job leads.

The importance of an informational call

Speaking to someone who works in a profession you've been considering isn't solely useful for aspiring Recruiters. Virtually everyone can benefit from these calls, as they'll have the chance to find out more about an industry, role, or even a specific company.

Furthermore, someone's firsthand account can be one of the most valuable pieces of information you receive during the research process. Though articles and videos are always useful, there's something to be said about conversing with a professional who can offer exclusive insights and personal opinions. Even if you *think* you know everything about the position, you're likely to come away with one — or a few — new bits of knowledge.

Of course, when it comes to the recruiting profession specifically, these benefits are even more useful. For instance, you might consider reaching out to an in-house, agency-based, and freelance Recruiter to receive a clearer idea of what each position entails and find out which one speaks to you most. They might even tell you whether *they* think you're a good fit for the type of recruitment they practice.

Sounds great, right? Now, let's look at how to set up these invaluable informational calls so you can get a head start on your career path.
How to find and talk to a Recruiter

Since most of your duties as a Recruiter will involve step-by-step processes, it only makes sense to start early. Keep in mind that you'll need to do some research on the career field before reaching out, though you should have a general basis developed after reading the previous chapters.

Finding a Recruiter to serve as your ally can be accomplished by following the formula below.

Researching potential interviewees

For this first step, you might want to pretend as if you're already a Recruiter searching for their next candidate — who *also* happens to be a Recruiter. Some ways to start your search include:

Starting with your own contacts

Do you have a friend, coworker, professor, or family member who knows someone in the recruitment field? Even if no one immediately comes to mind, it's worth asking your contacts if they can connect you with another professional. You never know who knows who!

Searching social media

Thanks to the wide availability of business-related social networks like LinkedIn, it's incredibly easy to find professionals in a field of your choosing with a simple online search. Even just one profile is usually enough to lead you to a long list of potential interviewees in the profession.

Contacting alumni

If you're currently attending or have attended a university, you might be able to access an online alumni database containing graduates from the school. As a bonus, those who appear in these searches have typically already agreed to speak with other alumnus about their job searching efforts. Even if they don't have time, they should be happy to refer you to someone else.

Researching industry leaders

This option is one of the most difficult and intimidating, but it's worth a shot and costs you nothing. Look into some of the leaders in the recruitment field, from the CEOs of established staffing agencies to the top-earning freelancers and consider reaching out to them. You might be surprised at who responds!

Remember that the quality of the information you receive depends on the quality of the people you interview, so take some time to ensure they're capable of granting you the insight you need to make the most informed decision.

Preparing for the interview

Found one or several people willing to talk to you about starting a new career in recruiting? Great! Now it's time to prepare.

While it's expected that the fellow Recruiter will be speaking the most, you should spend time preparing for the call. Not only will this ensure you walk away with all your questions answered, but it also shows you respect their time by coming into the interview with a game plan (something they might remember if they hear about a job opportunity!). This also includes catching up on your recruitment lingo and the latest trends within the industry.

Kicking things off

Once you've prepared for the interview and set up a time to have your call, the ball is in your court. It's fine to be a little nervous, but with a pre-determined strategy in mind, you'll find your groove in no time.

Here are some considerations to keep in mind for a smooth informational call:

Keep the introduction brief

Remember: This isn't a job interview. While it's customary to give a bit of backstory about yourself so the interviewee knows where you're coming from, try keeping it no longer than three minutes.

Perform an investigation

You might be happy to simply speak with someone who shares the same passion, but the main point is to come away with as much relevant information as possible. So, make sure you're gently feeding the interviewee questions throughout the call — though be careful not to come across as rude or disinterested in them as a person.

Show gratitude

Your interviewee has just blocked out time in their busy personal and professional lives to sit down and answer your questions, all for nothing in return. As such, they deserve some gratitude! Avoid making demands or asking for favors during the call and follow up with a thank-you e-mail once it's over (or, to make sure you're *really* remembered, a handwritten note!).

Build a relationship

Though you can certainly treat informational calls as a one-time thing, you'll receive much more value from them by considering it the beginning of a professional relationship.

Stay in contact with the interviewee and try doing something in return for them. Perhaps invite them to a networking event you're attending, send them links to articles you've found useful, and more. If there's a notable gap between your career progress, even just updating them about your achievements (and how their advice helped you get them) can be enough to maintain a mentor-like relationship.

As rare as it is, keep in mind that not every informational call will be perfect. Some interviewees could be resistant to answering your deeper questions, or you simply might learn something about a job that you weren't hoping to hear.

If this happens, it's not the end of the world. You'll just move onto the next professional on your list to collect alternative opinions and discover another point of view.

Chapter 7: How to Network for Recruiter Job Openings

Discussing different recruiting careers with a professional is invaluable, but it might also be slightly frustrating if you're hoping to land a role for yourself. You're talking to someone who probably heard about job openings weekly, yet you can't even ask them to throw one your way!

Well, you won't have to wait much longer — that's the next step.

At this point, you should be knowledgeable about recruiting and know where you want to fit into the industry. And, after scheduling a few informational calls, you'll be ready to start putting that knowledge into practice by searching for industry connections.

As with most things, the internet is going to be your number-one resource for discovering potential leads and connecting with people who can inform you about job openings. While conventional job postings on places like Indeed can lead you in a general direction, the "hidden" job market of referrals and professional networks is a much more effective (and quicker) way of landing a Recruiter position.

Let's look at how you can get started.

What networking is — and isn't

Networking has a few different definitions, depending on who you're speaking to. To the general public, this aspect of the professional world can seem slightly mysterious and even somewhat cynical.

Thanks to its portrayal in pop culture (think about movies like "The Wolf of Wall Street" or "The Social Network"), many assume "networking" is just a way for self-interested corporate henchmen to claw their way up the ladder, even if it means stepping on the heads of their colleagues.

Fortunately, this couldn't be further from the truth. While there are a small few who use networking to fuel their own interests without giving anything in return, these individuals don't make it very far in the game — and you'll see why.

At its core, networking is all about getting to know people. In fact, you do it every day when you talk to neighbors while cutting the lawn, speak to people at the grocery store, introduce yourself to people at local events, and more. Only, this time, the act is performed in a business setting with a fancier name attached to it.

Additionally, a focus of networking is to help others *while* helping yourself. By providing value to others, you'll inevitably receive something in return. It all relies on that basic, human connection we're all familiar with.

After enough time, you'll be able to recognize someone who's only in the game to benefit themselves and know to avoid them.

You can also expect the benefits of networking to blossom in a short amount of time, as people are generally happy to help others. Some of its major advantages include:

Improved employment chances

As a Recruiter, you'll soon discover that hiring managers are much more interested in professional relationships and referrals than cover letters and resumes. By networking, you'll grow a list of contacts who can inform you about job opportunities and put in a good word on your behalf.

Increased job opportunities

There are thousands of job postings uploaded online every day, yet these listings only scratch the surface of what lies underneath. Many times, employers are willing to fill a role long before they've ever drafted a job description or announced it, simply by searching for networking leads beforehand.

Reduced competition

Knowing just one person who works for a company you're applying to could work wonders, placing you ahead of the dozens of candidates who have yet to network with anyone in its workforce. Though it's not a guarantee you'll get hired, it certainly doesn't hurt your chances.

How to network in the recruiting field

The basics of networking are standard across all industries, which means your efforts to discover connections in the recruiting field can follow the same tried-

and-true methods used by thousands of other successful professionals.

Again, we're going to look at a step-by-step process to help you streamline your efforts and avoid wasted time.

Consider who you already know

Whether you realize it or not, you've already joined dozens of different networks in your lifetime. These could be related to sports teams, hobby clubs, friend groups, and more.

Since you're already familiar with these networks, this is often the easiest place to start your search. Even if you don't know someone who works as a Recruiter, there's no harm in asking your peers for potential leads. For instance, you might ask your child's teacher if there are any other parents in the school with the career or reach out to a college professor to ask about their professional contacts.

Though it might feel awkward at first, keep asking until you've exhausted every option available. Doing so could grant you access to various connections upfront, making the rest of the process much easier and saving hours of research. As a bonus, you'll have better luck establishing a professional connection with someone who has a mutual friend, compared to simply being a stranger.

After asking around your current network, you can begin browsing resources like LinkedIn, Facebook groups, and more to collect a list of people you'd like to speak with.

Know what you need

Before you start reaching out to the individuals on your list, take a step back and evaluate what you're hoping to gain from your networking efforts.

While it might seem as simple as collecting their e-mail and phone number, purpose-driven networking will yield the most success over time. This means going into it with a solid plan that covers who you want to speak to, why you want to speak to them, and what you'd like to come away with.

As such, it's wise to avoid the generic networking templates you'll find online. Though they're a good starting point that you can personalize, a cookie-cutter message might receive no reply if it contains little focus and doesn't tell the recipient what you're searching for.

To keep things clear, ensure you include some of the following information during your conversation:

Who you are: Even if you feel pressure to be perfect, avoid trying to be someone you are not. Authenticity is highly valued in all professional environments, especially in a field that relies so heavily on interpersonal communication and collaboration. Along with your best, true self, don't forget to mention your qualifications and professional experience.

What advice you need: Just like in your informational calls, you shouldn't treat networking like a direct job search. Instead, simply ask for advice and — more importantly — offer something in return. You want to make an ally in the field who, if the opportunity comes their way, might inform you about a job opening at some point in the future.

What your goals are: Of course, most people know networking is more than casual conversation. As nice as it is to speak with someone in the same field, it's mainly a way to achieve something. So, be sure you know what that "something" is for you. Maybe you need a reference, insight into a specific career path, or the contact information of another professional.

As always, all of this should come from a courteous, respectful place. No matter how experienced you might be, having the wrong attitude could rub people the wrong way and convince them to pass their opportunities to another contact instead.

Use software tools to your advantage

As a Recruiter, you'll be working with many kinds of software to power your duties, from AI resume tools to collaboration-focused solutions. So, why not use the networking step to practice your tech skills?

There are a few great extensions available specifically designed for modern job hunting, which will only improve your chances of securing a role when paired with your networking efforts.

Mailtrack – E-mail tracker for Gmail

Ever wanted to pull your hair out wondering if your e-mails were read by a hiring manager, or went straight to their spam folder? Mailtrack is a free extension that tells you everything you need to know through comprehensive e-mail analytics, notifying you whenever your e-mails are opened.

Todoist — Organization tool for Chrome

It's easy to lose track of all the documents and pages you'll come across during your job search. Todoist can keep it all organized by labeling daily assignments, saving items to a reading list, reminding you to follow-up on tasks, and more.

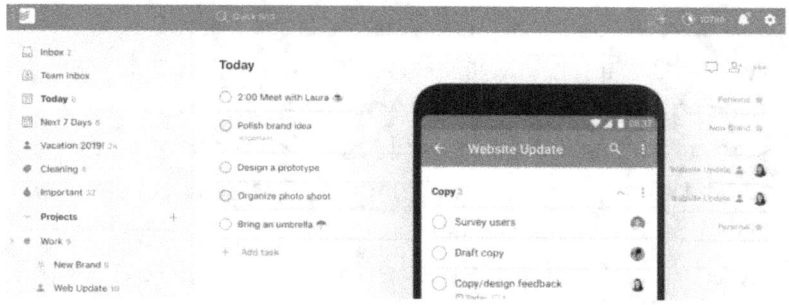

StayFocused

As the name suggests, this extension keeps you from wandering off to social media and other time-wasting websites in the middle of your job search.

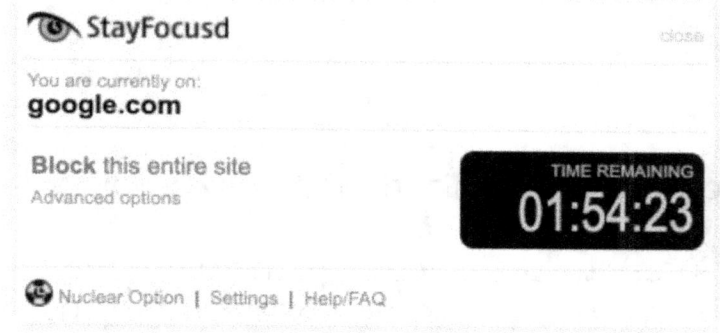

LinkedIn Recruiter Extension

If you want to be notified of every message received on your LinkedIn profile, the network's extension will keep you up to date on all activity related to your account.

Huntr – Job Search Tracker

Keeping job postings organized might be one of the most difficult parts of the process, which is why Huntr is designed to help aspiring workers keep track of their results.

Focus on the human connection

If you ever feel intimidated by the prospect of networking, remember that it's something you've done almost every day since you were born. Focus on building authentic, meaningful connections that provide value to others. In return, opportunities will eventually find themselves on your doorstep (or inbox) without requiring you to lift a finger.

Chapter 8: How to Land an Entry Recruiter Role with No Experience

Having any doubts yet? At this point, there might be a few swirling in your head. Things like:

- **"Am I experienced enough?"**
- **"Who will hire me as a beginner?"**
- **"Should I just give up now?"**

Don't panic; these are completely normal. In fact, these fears aren't only felt by aspiring Recruiters.

Almost everyone has felt insecure about their professional experience at some point, whether they're applying for a temporary position at a local mom-and-pop shop or a leading role at a multinational corporation. Still, everyone once had to start from nothing before working their way up — yes, even the CEO of that Fortune 100 company who you've always admired.

And, since starting a career with little or no experience is such a universal experience, there are a few proven steps you can follow to improve your chances of landing an entry Recruiter role.

How to sell yourself with no experience

Identify and highlight your soft skills

Everyone has at least *one* skill they can highlight, whether they've been working for decades or just a few months. Until you've developed skills specific to a certain profession or industry, these general abilities (also known as "soft skills") will prove you have the potential for growth.

Some of these include:

- ✓ Problem-solving
- ✓ Organization
- ✓ Communication
- ✓ Time management
- ✓ Interpersonal skills
- ✓ Leadership
- ✓ Creativity
- ✓ Adaptability
- ✓ Collaboration

If you completed the Strengths Finder Assessment mentioned in Chapter 1, you should already have a few of these in mind.

Emphasize transferable experience

Changing careers can be daunting, especially if your previous one is unrelated to the corporate world. However, you should look at this as an advantage rather than a disadvantage, since it means you can prove how you previously utilized your soft skills in a working environment.

So, think hard about your past positions and the way they could relate to a Recruiter's duties, regardless of how different they might be.

For example, if you previously worked a customer service job, you likely had to focus on interpersonal, communication, and management skills daily. Consider problems you had to solve on the fly, organization methods you practiced, and more.

Understand your motivations

Most employers want to know *why* you're interested in a job regardless of your experience level, though the question is most common for entry-level positions.

Without any experience in the field, a hiring manager could ask you to talk about your motivations for applying. Since "for the money" isn't a great answer, it's worth taking some time to look at your personal reasons for following the recruitment path.

For instance, do you love working in a team environment? Are you passionate about helping others land the right career? Have you always wanted to work in a corporate field? All the above?

By applying to jobs with these reasons pre-established, you'll come across as knowledgeable about the profession — and confident that you'll succeed in it.

Start applying

Now comes the part you've been preparing for: Applying for the Recruiter role you've always dreamt about.

If you've spent a few weeks networking beforehand, you might already know about some available roles. If not, start searching for job postings using the software mentioned in the previous chapter.

Even if the little voice in your head tells you you're not qualified enough, apply for the listings you find anyways. You'll be surprised at how many employers would like to learn more about you and what you bring to the table.

As always, remember to follow best practices when making your resume and cover letters, placing emphasis on your transferable experience and soft skills.

Prepare for the interview

Congratulations! You've made an impression with your application and heard back from a Recruiter who wants to speak with you about the role.

It's normal for nerves to set in, but they can easily be reduced through proper preparation.

Even if they're reworded, many Recruiters ask the same tried-and-true questions to evaluate their candidates, meaning you can start practicing long in advance. A few common ones you should expect to answer include:

- Why do you want to become a Recruiter?
- How would you use data to help recruit highly qualified professionals?
- What steps does it take to create a successful talent pipeline?
- Which traits are the most important for a Recruiter to develop?
- What would you do if a candidate rejected your job offer?
- How would you help make the company a top choice for potential candidates?
- What steps would you take to work with a hiring manager who was hard to please?
- How do you stay on top of the latest recruitment trends and developments?

Additionally, *you'll* want to ask your own questions at the end of the interview. Not only will this create a great impression by showcasing your attentiveness and passion for the role, but it'll also supply you with exclusive information you can use in future interviews. Consider the following.

What traits and methods do your most successful Recruiters share?

What are the most common challenges your company's Recruiters face?
Which recruitment solutions and ATS systems do your Recruiters use?
How does your company evaluate its Recruiters' success rate?

Additional interview tips

There's no such thing as too much preparation before an interview, so be sure you're doing all you can to set yourself up for success. Review the following bonus tips to increase your chance of nailing the conversation.

Keep your resume relevant

Even if you're applying to multiple entry-level recruitment roles, it's wise to adapt your resume for each application. Some companies might focus on different skills, which you can make a point to highlight in your materials.

Don't forget about etiquette

Showing up on time, dressing professionally, and having the right attitude are just as important as work experience and qualifications. Don't be afraid to let your personality shine and showcase your excitement for the position!

Show off a bit: Some candidates might feel shy about sharing their accomplishments in fear of coming across as arrogant or too entitled, but this typically isn't how Recruiters will see it — that is, unless you *are* arrogant or too entitled. So, be ready to talk about your professional skills and how they've helped you earn your current achievements.

Practice, practice, practice

Set up a mock interview with a friend to help you visualize the meeting, verbalize your answers succinctly, and take off the edge.

Showcase your knowledge

Once it's time for your interview, you've likely already spent hours researching the position, the company, the Recruiter, and more. Be ready to show you've done your homework with your answers.

Chapter 9: How to Ramp Up Your Recruiting Career

Once you've successfully landed your first recruiting job, it won't be long before your workload begins ramping up as you begin overseeing applications, speaking to candidates, collaborating with hiring managers, and more.

Eventually, things can start to get overwhelming. That is, if you're not prepared for what's to come.

By now, you've probably realized that recruitment duties are fast paced by nature. Even if you're working as an in-house Recruiter with a smaller workload, the company relies on you to keep its workforce supplied with a consistent flow of quality employees.

So, rather than allowing these tasks to pile on your shoulders and weigh you down, you should be ready to face them head-on with confidence. In this chapter, we'll go over the main skills and methods you'll use to take control of your career.

Skill development

Though you might've come into your position with a few pre-earned skills at your disposal, you'll simply find yourself learning more and more with each day. Don't let these opportunities to expand your capabilities pass by — reel them in and use them for self-improvement.

So, what should you focus on mastering early on? (Spoiler: You can probably already think of a few!)

Communication

Not a big surprise, is it? Communication skills are at the forefront of your efforts and can *always* be improved, especially with the number of evolving solutions on the market.

Flexibility

The modern business is in a constant state of change. From remote work to the four-day workweek, you'll need to know how to adapt to new situations without reducing the quality of your output.

Time management

Recruiters always have a task to complete, whether they're focusing on solely one part of the full cycle process or the entire thing. If you haven't already, learning how to manage your time efficiently is a must.

Self-analysis

The best Recruiters know how to evaluate their personal progress, identify areas that require improvement, and identify solutions to help them keep growing.

Patience

Burnout is part of the "ugly truth" behind recruiting, as it can be discouraging to encounter multiple rejected job offers in a row, or simply have trouble sourcing the right candidate. Don't forget to take care of yourself and know how to calm yourself down if you feel overwhelmed.

Creativity

Not every problem related to recruitment can be solved using algorithms and data. Since you're in the "people" business, you'll also need to have a level of empathy and creativity to help you solve workplace issues and soothe candidate worries.

Habit creation

No matter how much you've dreamt, researched, and prepared for a new job position, there's always a level of shock that comes with the experience. This short period is a crucial chance for you to create healthy habits that set you up for success.

Creating a solid routine is the best way to avoid troubles early in the process and show your managers you're more than just talk. Of course, routine building is easier said than done, though it'll fall into place automatically if you're consciously making decisions for maximum efficiency.

Some habits maintained by top performers across the industry include:

- Scheduling phone calls in place of e-mails
- Asking relevant, productive questions (one at a time)
- Staying up to date on the latest changes and trends in the industry
- Keeping it human — even corporate leaders can have fun
- Keep track of who you speak with

After enough time, these habits will become second nature to you. Along the way, think about some other ones you could include in your routine related to your specific company and position.

Mentorship

By now, you know that finding and maintaining a job isn't a one-person effort. Along the way, you relied on relationships formed during your networking stage to find a role, received expert advice through informational calls, asked important questions during your interviews, and more.

Still, the benefits provided by professional connections don't stop as soon as you accept a job offer. In fact, they've only just started.

Moving forward, your next task will be to find a mentor in your field. If you went to college, you might compare the role to an academic advisor. Though they aren't there to hold your hand through *every* step of your career, they'll be a valuable resource to turn to when you find yourself needing insight and advice regarding certain situations, paths, and strategies only an expert would know.

Along with this, they'll help you build additional relationships in the industry and are often willing to write you strong letters of recommendation for future positions. Furthermore, simply having an outsider watch your journey from start to finish can grant you a new perspective when evaluating what has and hasn't been working.

And, since you're no longer a stranger to networking, you should have an idea of where to start. So, once you're ready, it's time to begin your search by following these steps.

Outline your mentorship goals

Both you and your mentor will need to know what you hope to use the relationship for to be as productive as possible. Outline a few goals and think about how a mentor could help you achieve them.

Know what to say

Whether you're reaching out to a pre-established professional connection or a stranger, make sure you spend time drafting your "elevator pitch." This should include the goals you've just defined, why you want them to be your mentor, and how you hope they can help your career.

Start reaching out

You can find mentors using one of the many networking methods we've already gone over: i.e., through LinkedIn, your personal network, professional associations you belong to, your own workplace, and more.

Schedule a meeting

Save e-mail as a last resort. A one-on-one meeting or call with the other person will help you explain your objectives much clearer and grant them the opportunity to ask questions.

Maintain contact

Once you've found someone who's agreed to be your mentor, you can look forward to a long relationship that grants both parties incredible value. Still, to keep it from becoming stagnant, you'll have to maintain contact with them.

How you do this depends on your schedules and goals. You might schedule meetings once a week or once a month, for instance. Avoid confusion by discussing a schedule during your initial meeting — and stick to it.
Long-term growth

One of the most exciting aspects about the recruitment field is its extensive potential for personal and professional growth. You'll always be learning something new, working with different people, and encountering challenges that might not yet have a solution. With a growth-oriented mindset, these factors will simply be another chance to improve workplace skills.

For some, this might seem intimidating. For those meant for the role, it should sound like a thrilling opportunity.

Chapter 10: Conducting an Intake Meeting

You'll likely start encountering intake meetings shortly after settling into a recruitment role, which is one of the main steps in the full cycle process.

As part of the "preparation" stage, it is a chance for the Recruiter and hiring manager to discuss the open position and outline crucial information such as:

- ✓ Criteria regarding candidate qualifications
- ✓ The job's title
- ✓ The job's duties
- ✓ The hiring stages candidates will go through

As you can see, intake meetings are incredibly important, as it grants the Recruiter everything, they need to start creating a hiring plan. Additionally, it allows them to engage with the hiring manager early in the recruiting process, eliminating hiccups and miscommunications long before the first applicant interview is ever scheduled.

How do Recruiters prepare for intake meetings?

Researching the role

Even if the hiring manager is coming to the table with the majority of the information, Recruiters can save time and reduce back-and-forth after the meeting by performing preliminary research.

To set themselves up for success, most will try to find answers to the following questions before attending an intake meeting:

1. What kind of salary benchmark does the position have?
2. Which qualifications and skills would a good candidate need to be successful in the role?
3. How much time will the Recruiter require for each hiring stage?
4. What kind of metrics might be used in the recruiting process (i.e., yield ratios, time-to-fill, time-to-hire)?
5. Has the finance team set a recruitment budget for the role?
6. Is the role a long-term or temporary position?

7. Will the candidate be replacing a previous employee or filling a new role?

Outlining questions

It's rare for a Recruiter to find answers to *everything* before the intake meeting. Fortunately, that's exactly what it's for!

Your hiring manager will expect you to have a few inquiries to help you better understand what kind of candidate they're looking for. Some common questions include:

- Why do they need to fill the role?
- What function does their department oversee for the company?
- What responsibilities and contributions will the new hire be expected to satisfy?
- Which qualifications and skills are "must-haves", and which ones are simply "nice-to-haves"?
- How much experience would a good candidate need to have? Must the experience be directly related to the role?

- What is the expected compensation range for the role? What benefits and perks will it include?
- How soon would a new hire need to start?
- Are there any deal breakers that could automatically eliminate a candidate?

Use these as a starting point when drafting your questions. Customize them according to your specific situation or create your own.

What do Recruiters do during an intake meeting?

After they've done a fair amount of preparation, Recruiters should be ready to hold their intake meeting with the hiring manager. This is where the magic happens, and everything is laid out to ensure both parties are ready to begin the hiring process.

As such, what a Recruiter *does* during the meeting is fairly straightforward: collect as much information as they need — possibly even a little more.

What do Recruiters do after an intake meeting?

Communication between the Recruiter and hiring manager doesn't end after the intake meeting. Be prepared to stay in contact regarding a few follow-up tasks.

Answering additional questions

No matter how much information they collected during the meeting, it's normal for the Recruiter to have at least *one* more question they need answered. The hiring manager will likely have a few as well.

Status updates

Even if a Recruiter is solely overseeing "recruitment" for the role, most of their efforts operate in tandem with the hiring manager. Throughout the hiring process, they'll need to send them regular status updates and reports generated by their Applicant Tracking System (ATS). Doing so will limit confusion and ensure the relationship is as smooth as possible.

Creating job postings

Depending on the company and role, either the Recruiter, hiring manager, or both will be responsible for drafting the job description — one for internal use, and the other for external advertising (i.e., online job boards like Indeed).

Helping with interviews

Some hiring managers will ask for another pair of hands to help them with their interview strategy. The Recruiter might help them draft questions (especially if they're not sure which questions are legal and illegal), review candidates' answers, and more.

Creating a successful relationship with a hiring manager

Even if you prefer to work alone, Recruiters should be willing to invest time in their relationship with the hiring manager. Doing so will only benefit your efforts and keep things running smoothly from start to finish.

So, keep the next four steps in mind as you prepare to work with your hiring manager.

Meet with them often

You're probably sick of hearing about communication by now, but there's a reason why I've mentioned it so many times throughout this book: it *works*.

Sure, the thought of adding one more task to your plate might be a hard pill to swallow. However, if you look at the big picture, the benefits speak for themselves. Even just a 30-minute meeting with your hiring manager could squash a future problem that would've taken hours to solve.

Be prepared

Every professional — not just hiring managers — appreciates working with someone who's done their homework.

As mentioned earlier, you'll want to approach a new hiring manager with preliminary research that proves you've prepared in advance. That means researching their open role, looking up terms related to the position and industry, exploring skills they might look for in a candidate, and more.

Be transparent

As easy as it would make it, hiring managers can't read your mind. Though you might be hyper-focused on your work and eager to get things started, understand that they might not yet be on the same page.

So, take a step back and check-in regularly to tell the hiring manager about your current efforts, progress, and future plans regarding the hiring process. Outline specific data they might find useful and consider whether they might be overwhelmed at any point.

By being readily available to answer questions and being transparent about your plans, you can minimize confusion and show the hiring manager you're someone who can be trusted.

Ask for feedback

Accepting criticism isn't always easy, especially when it comes to your field of work. Recruiters need to let go of any ego getting in their way and be willing to ask hiring managers for feedback about their performance.

Their answers shouldn't be taken as an insult. In fact, they're giving you a clear outline to follow to prevent future problems and ensure your energy is being well spent.

As a result, you'll make the hiring manager more willing to accept feedback in return.

Chapter 11: Talent Sourcing & Searching 101

Your intake meeting and preparations are a crucial aspect of the hiring process, yet they won't yield any results on their own. For that, you'll have to finally begin searching for candidates to fit the role you've been tasked with.

Fortunately, this is something that Recruiters have been doing for decades, which means you can rely on their pre-established strategies — though with a modern twist.

Still, despite the number of solutions and resources that promise to help you discover top candidates without needing to lift a finger, it's important to maintain focus during this step. Talent sourcing is the "make or break" moment, as your candidate pool will depend on where, how, and when you search for applicants.

Don't worry; It takes practice, but this is another skill that can be developed and sharpened with time. To get started, you'll need to know the basics.

Talent sourcing tools

If you've previously researched the recruiting profession on your own, you might've seen ATS and CRM systems mentioned a few times. Let's examine each to pinpoint what makes them different and — more importantly — the roles they'll play in your efforts.

What is an ATS?

Applicant Tracking Software is a major resource most Recruiters use throughout the hiring process. Both they and hiring managers will use it throughout their efforts to write and post job openings, receive and organize their applications, and move candidates through hiring stages.

What is a CRM?

A Candidate Relationship Management system is designed to strengthen potential candidates' and Recruiters' connections so that Recruiters may use them for future job opportunities. Because of this, CRMs are considered a major component of most recruitment efforts, enabling professionals to build talent communities and maintain ties with inactive candidates. As such, when it's time to hire someone new, Recruiters will already have a group of pre-vetted prospects from which they can choose.

Which is best for Recruiters?

Essentially, Recruiters use CRMs to scale their sourcing efforts by attracting passive candidates ahead of time. Meanwhile, ATSs are designed to make selection and hiring as simple as possible by eliminating needless administrative activities and improving workflow. As such, you'll most likely find yourself relying on both as a Recruiter.

Talent sourcing basics

Regardless of what company you're working with, there are a few standards hiring managers expect Recruiters to follow when talent sourcing.

Start with your applicant tracking software

The first place you should start your search is in your ATS. If you've been hired to fill a role, the hiring manager will likely have already created a job opening and included specific instructions on how they want it filled. Review the job opening and look for keywords related to the position that you can use to help focus your search.

Search for potential candidates on social media

Once you have a good idea of what you're looking for, it's time to widen the net and start searching social media platforms like LinkedIn, Twitter, and Facebook. Recruiters often use these sites to find passive candidates — people who aren't necessarily looking for new opportunities but may be interested in applying for a position when given the chance.

Attend job fairs and conferences

Job fairs and industry conferences are another great place to meet potential candidates. Attendees are usually eager to learn about new opportunities, and many Recruiters take the opportunity to hand out business cards or even do on-the-spot interviews.

Check with your professional network

Your professional network can be a valuable resource when it comes to finding talent. Ask friends, family members, or former colleagues if they know anyone who would be a good fit for the role you're trying to fill.

Use social media ads

If you want to increase your candidate pool even further, consider using social media ads. Of course, this isn't a free option, which means you'll need to discuss cost restrictions with your hiring manager. But, if you have the budget, social media ads can be a great way to find qualified job seekers you might've otherwise missed out on.

Tweak your outreach strategy

Now that you have a good idea of where to find potential candidates, it's time to focus on how to reach out to them in a way that will pique their interest.
When writing your outreach messages, be sure to:

Address the candidate by name
Mention the specific role you're trying to fill
Include a short, customized message about why you think the candidate would be a good fit for the position.

Make it easy for the candidate to respond (include your contact information and a link to your online application)

Utilize Boolean search strings

A Boolean string is a search term that uses Boolean modifiers and operators (AND, OR, and (-) NOT) to narrow or broaden your search results when attempting to discover talent through Google searches.

For example, if you want to find candidates who have experience with Salesforce AND have a degree in marketing, you will use the following Boolean string:

"Salesforce" AND "CRM"

The OR operator tells the ATS system to look for candidates with experience in either one of the two keywords. If you wanted to find candidates who have either experience with Salesforce or marketing, you would use this Boolean string:

("Salesforce" OR "CRM" OR "Cloud")

You can also use OR to continue expanding your search results, which is especially useful for synonyms. Using the example above, you might type something like:

("Salesforce" OR "marketing" OR "business administration")

Finally, the NOT (-) operator excludes any results that include the keyword after the NOT. So, this string would return candidates who have experience with marketing but do not have experience with Salesforce:

-"Salesforce"

Here's some more examples to search for resumes online:

(inurl:resume OR intitle:resume) filetype:PDF

(intitle:resume OR intitle:cv) (filetype:pdf OR filetype:doc OR filetype:txt)

(resume OR cv) filetype:pdf

(intitle:resume OR inurl:resume OR intitle:cv OR inurl:cv OR intitle:vitae OR inurl:vitae)

(intitle:resume OR inurl:resume OR intitle:cv OR inurl:cv OR intitle:vitae OR inurl:vitae OR intitle:bio OR inurl:bio OR intitle:profile OR inurl:profile)

(intitle:resume OR inurl:resume OR intitle:bio OR inurl:bio OR intitle:vitae OR inurl:vitae OR intitle:cv OR inurl:cv OR intitle:homepage OR inurl:homepage)

"download my cv|resume" gmail.com

pdf|doc|docx gmail.com intitle:resume | inurl:resume

I recommend reading my other book titled: *Boolean Basics for Recruiters* for more examples.

Keep learning

No matter how long you've been in the game, you'll continue to learn new strategies and tools that can help you source talent better than ever. So, keep an eye out for these educational opportunities as you continue to expand your skills, and take note of the methods that seem to work for you — as well as those that don't.

Chapter 12: Writing Job Descriptions & Posting Jobs Online

So, you've finally received your first job that you need to create a posting for and publish online.

Again, this is another crucial aspect of the recruitment process, as this will be the first impression potential candidates have of your company. You not only want to find the best talent, but you also want to represent your company in the best possible way.

There are a few strategies you can use to your advantage to ensure your posting is as attractive as possible, which we'll go over in this chapter. But first, it's time for some review.

What is a job posting?

Job postings are often made up of four main sections: the headline, the overview, the qualifications, and the contact information.

Headline

The headline is your opportunity to hook potential candidates with a catchy phrase or sentence. It should be concise and to-the-point, as it will be one of the first things people see when browsing through job postings.

Overview

The overview section is where you give a brief summary of what the job is and what kind of person would be a good fit for it. This section should be around 100-200 words long.

Qualifications

The qualifications section is where you list the specific skills and experience that are required for the position. For instance, if you're searching for an IT professional, you might ask for knowledge regarding certain software programs or operating systems.

Contact Information

Here, you'll provide the necessary details for people who are interested in applying for the position. This should include the company's name, address, e-mail address, and website.

How to write a job posting

Now that we've covered the basics, let's take a look at some tips for writing an effective job posting.

Focus on the candidate

When writing your job posting, it's important to remember that you're not just selling your company — you're also selling the position itself. This means that you need to focus on what the position can offer the candidate, rather than what they can offer the company.

Detail some of the things they'll look forward to when joining the company. Include perks like a great benefits package, a fun company culture, or opportunities for professional development.

Talk about the job

Of course, no applicant will want to spend time drafting a resume and cover letter for a position they have zero knowledge about. That's why it's important to include a detailed overview of the job, including the responsibilities and duties involved.

This will give potential candidates a good idea of what they can expect if they are hired for the position. It will also help them determine if they are a good fit for the role.

You'll want to be as specific as possible in this section without overcomplicating things. It might help to imagine describing the job to a friend who simply wants to know what a day-in-the-life would look like.

List the qualifications

As I mentioned earlier, one of the most important aspects of a job posting is listing the qualifications required for the position. This will help you narrow down your pool of candidates and ensure that you're only considering people who have the skills and experience necessary for the job.

Use keywords

One of the best ways to attract qualified candidates is by using keywords in your job posting. These are words and phrases that are related to the position you're hiring for, so make sure to use them throughout your post.

As a bonus, this will also help candidates who are looking for specific jobs find your listing more easily when performing their own search.

Don't forget the details

You never know how many other job postings a candidate has reviewed before landing on yours. Providing as many crucial details as possible upfront will help to avoid any confusion or misunderstandings further down the line. Some of these include:

Pay: Let candidates know what the salary range is for the position.
Location: If the job is remote, state that in the posting.
Start date: Let applicants know when you plan to start interviewing and hiring.
Application process: Let candidates know what the next steps are in the application process (the shorter, the better!).

Use images sparingly

While images can be a great way to add visual appeal to your job posting, it's important not to go overboard. Too many images can make your post difficult to read and could cause candidates to lose interest.

Choose one or two images that will help illustrate the position you're hiring for. Make sure they are high-quality and relevant to the content of your post.

Avoid gender bias

Including gender-based language in your job posting can be a major turnoff for potential candidates. It's important to avoid words like "female" or "male" when describing the ideal candidate, and instead use terms like "person" or "individual."

Keep in mind that other examples of gender bias can be entirely unconscious. For example, if you use a gendered word to describe a desirable personality trait (e.g., "confident"), try to find a more inclusive alternative. Check out [Joblint.org] for a list of "masculine" and "feminine" words to avoid leaning too heavily in one direction.

It's also worth asking a gender-diverse panel to review your posting to receive their feedback on its inclusivity. Remember: Recruiting and hiring a more diverse talent pool will only help your company or client succeed in the long term.

Seek feedback

It's always a good idea to seek feedback from others before posting a job opening. Ask your team members, friends, or even family members to read over the post and provide their honest thoughts.

This can help you catch any mistakes or areas that could be improved. Plus, it's always helpful to get a fresh perspective! Where to post jobs

There are several different places to post jobs, depending on what type of position you're hiring for. Here are a few popular options:

LinkedIn

This is a great starting point for Recruiters looking to hire employees for almost any professional role, as it allows you to search for candidates based on their skills, job title, or company.

Indeed

Since this popular site is 100% free for job seekers, you'll find a large talent pool already waiting for you to dive into.

Zip Recruiter

This option is especially helpful for small businesses or startups that don't have the time or resources to conduct a large-scale recruiting campaign. Zip Recruiter allows you to post your job opening and then searches through its database of candidates to find the best fit for your position.

Monster

This website is a popular place for businesses that are looking to fill mid- to senior-level positions. Monster allows you to post your job opening and then searches through its database of candidates to find the best fit for your position.

Social media

Platforms like Twitter and Facebook can be used to post jobs, though they may not be as popular as some of the other options listed above.

Understanding OFCCP Employment Guidelines

If you're recruiting for a federal contractor, you must also be aware of the Office of Federal Contractor Compliance Programs' (OFCCP) employment guidelines, which center around three main laws:

Executive Order (E.O.) 11246 bans discrimination in employment and requires affirmative action to guarantee that all employment decisions are made without regard to race, color, religion, sex, sexual orientation, gender identity, or national origin.

The Rehabilitation Act of 1973, as amended by the Workforce Innovations Act of 1998, prohibits discrimination, and requires employers to take active steps to hire qualified disabled individuals.

The Vietnam Era Veterans' Readjustment Assistance Act (VEVRA) prohibits veterans protected by the Act from being discriminated against and requires employers to take active steps to recruit and hire them.

Complying with the OFCCP is fairly straightforward, as the organization largely focuses on:

Ensuring employers aren't discriminating against employees or applicants on the basis of their color, race, sex, religion, national origin, sexual orientation, or gender identity.

Taking affirmative action to prevent employees from being treated with any regard to their color, race, sex, religion, national origin, sexual orientation, or gender identity.

As a Recruiter, it's important that your postings comply with OFCCP regulations, so you may want to seek the help of a compliance officer to ensure this is the case. To stay within the guidelines, they'll need to:

Use specific language absent of discrimination

Offer an online application process accessible to disabled individuals
Describe the company's commitment to equal opportunity, regardless of an applicant's color, race, sex, religion, national origin, sexual orientation, or gender identity

Getting started

These are just a few standard steps to get you started, but there are many other tips to make your job posting stand out — a majority of which you'll pick up simply through experience. Still, by following these guidelines, you'll be able to create an effective post that will help you find the perfect candidate for any open position.

Chapter 13: Social Media, Recruitment Marketing, & Employment Branding

Recruiting has evolved considerably in the last decade. In order to hire the best employees, firms must expand their numbers rapidly without sacrificing quality. Of course, thanks to shifting landscapes, this is a challenge that only grows more difficult over time.

As such, recruitment marketing and social media has become an increasingly important piece of the puzzle. Though things like job postings are a classic, straightforward way to land top talent, Recruiters need to start thinking about the bigger picture. While these strategies can still be part of your toolset, is there another, newer method you can look into to stay ahead of the curve?

To give you a head start, let's explore how these newer approaches work and how they can benefit your recruitment efforts moving forward.

What is recruitment marketing?

Put simply, recruitment marketing is the practice of promoting your employer brand to attract top talent. It encompasses all marketing activities aimed at increasing awareness of your company as an employer and convincing potential candidates that your business is a great place to work.

The most successful recruitment marketers focus on creating a strong content strategy that engages candidates on a personal level. This might include sharing photos and stories from current employees, highlighting unique company culture elements, or showcasing exciting new projects in the works.

In addition, savvy Recruiters make use of social media platforms like LinkedIn, Twitter, and Facebook to reach out to potential candidates directly — also known as social recruiting.

What is social recruiting?

Social recruiting is the process of finding and engaging potential candidates through social media platforms. It involves identifying active and passive job seekers, building relationships with them, and enticing them to consider your company as a future employer.

The best way to think about social recruiting is as an extension of your existing recruitment marketing strategy. Rather than simply posting job openings on your website or LinkedIn page, you can use social media to actively reach out to potential candidates and connect with them on a more personal level.

Now, why is social recruiting important? Well, social media has become an integral part of our lives. In fact, it's now rare to find someone who doesn't have at least *one* account on a platform. As such, it's the number-one source for making connections outside of the real world. That means if you're not active on social media, you're likely missing out on a large pool of potential candidates.

But it's not just about numbers. The other benefit of social recruiting is that it allows you to build relationships with potential candidates before they even apply. This can give you a competitive edge over other employers, since candidates are more likely to choose a company that they feel has a personal connection with them.

What is employment branding?

Recruitment marketing and social media/social recruiting all work towards one main goal: employment branding. Essentially, this is the process of creating a positive image of your company as an employer.

Of course, there are quite a few factors that go into employment branding that you might not interact with as a Recruiter, such as overall company culture, but it's a good idea to keep the company's overarching branding goals in mind when developing your recruitment strategy.

Social recruiting strategies

Now that we've covered the basics, let's see how you can start using social media to recruit top talent.

Know which platforms to use

Not all social media platforms are created equal when it comes to recruiting. LinkedIn, for example, is the best platform for targeting active and passive job seekers, while Twitter is great for reaching out to potential candidates directly.

Additionally, different demographics tend to migrate to separate channels. A visual designer, for instance, will likely have a larger presence on TikTok or Pinterest, whereas a software engineer might spend most of their time on LinkedIn or Reddit.

Make applying easy

One of the main goals of social recruiting is to get potential candidates interested enough in your company to apply. One way to do this is by making the application process as easy as possible. This might mean including a link to an online application on your social media posts, or even setting up a chatbot that can help candidates with the application process.

Build relationships with potential candidates

The best way to get potential candidates interested in your company or open position is by building relationships with them. You can do this by following them on social media, commenting on their posts, and sharing their content.

Even if they don't land the role, you'll have made a connection you can immediately turn to for future openings.

Take advantage of built-in recruitment tools

Most social media platforms have recognized the part they play in the hiring process and are providing tools specifically for job seekers and Recruiters alike.

LinkedIn, for example, offers several features to help you find and connect with potential candidates, such as its Recruiter tool and Talent Insights. Facebook also has a number of tools for businesses looking to hire, including its Jobs tab and Interview Kit.

So, investigate each platform to make sure you're taking advantage of all the tools it has available!

Create content that engages potential candidates

Finally, creating engaging content that speaks to candidates' interests is another powerful strategy. This might include blog posts about the latest industry trends, infographics about the benefits of working at your company, or even videos of current employees talking about why they love their job.

Review

Social recruiting is the process of using social media to identify and attract potential candidates for a job opening. Recruiters use social media to build relationships with potential candidates before they even apply, making it easier for them to choose their company over others.

Additionally, most platforms provide tools specifically for job seekers and Recruiters, making the process even easier on both sides.

Chapter 14: Time management Tips for Recruiters

It's safe to say that, as a Recruiter, you'll have quite the busy workload. From managing calls to scheduling interviews to sorting through resumes, long periods of downtime are usually a rare occurrence.

With so much on your plate, it's crucial to manage your time well. Poor time management can lead to missed deadlines, lower quality work, and even burnout. Over time, this'll reduce your ability to source top talent and reduce a company's willingness to work with you for their hiring needs.

But not all is lost. By following the best practices for time management when it comes to recruiting, you can avoid disaster and keep productivity at an all-time high.

Best time management habits:

Create a to-do list

This one is a no-brainer, but it's still worth mentioning.

When you have a lot of tasks to complete, it can be helpful to have them all written down in one place. This gives you a visual representation of what still needs to be done and allows for easy prioritization.

It's also important to make sure your list is realistic. Don't try to cram too many items into a short time frame, as this will only lead to frustration and decreased productivity.

Schedule your time

In addition to creating a to-do list, it's helpful to schedule out your time as well. This means that you'll know exactly when you're supposed to be working on each task and will be less likely to get sidetracked along the way.

Considering the bigger picture, it's also worth creating a calendar for the month where you can plot deadlines, planned meetings, and more. Don't forget to check off completed tasks when they're done to keep it organized! I use calendar blocking techniques daily to effectively manage my routines. Blocking 2-3 hours to source on a given day will help you stay focused on your main goal – which ultimately is to make a hire placement.

Take breaks

Believe it or not, taking breaks is actually a key part of good time management. When you're constantly working on something, your brain can start to feel overwhelmed. This can lead to decreased productivity and errors.

By taking short breaks throughout the day — whether for 5 minutes or half an hour – you'll grant your brain a chance to reset. This'll make it easier to focus when you do get back to work and will decrease the likelihood of making mistakes.

Use productivity software

There are several different productivity software programs out there, and they can be a lifesaver when it comes to time management. Programs like Asana or Trello allow you to create tasks, set deadlines, and track progress. This way, you always know what still needs to be done and can avoid overlap in tasks.

Additionally, these programs often have built-in reminders, so you never forget an important task, such as an upcoming interview or a phone call you still need to return.

Don't forget to allot personal time

Even if you're good at managing your time, it's important to schedule in some personal time as well. This could be anything from taking a walk outside to watching your favorite show on Netflix.

When you're constantly working, it's easy to let it take over your life, especially if you're operating on a freelance basis. But by scheduling in some personal time, you're ensuring that you'll still have energy to give your best when it matters most.

Avoid distractions

We all know that distractions can be a major time-sink. From checking Facebook notifications to answering work e-mails outside of office hours, there are plenty of ways for them to sneak in.

To avoid being pulled off track, it's important to have a plan. This could mean designating specific times of day for responding to e-mails or turning off your phone notifications altogether. If you're working from home, it might also be helpful to set up a specific workspace where you can focus on your tasks without any interruptions.

Track your accomplishments

At the end of every week, take a few minutes to track your accomplishments. This could be anything from landing a new client to completing a project on time. Not only will this give you a sense of satisfaction, but it'll also show you what you're capable of and boost your reputation.

Create a KPI sourcing tracker document that tracks all your outreaches, phone screen calls, and submittals every week. You can reference this if your hiring manager or recruiting manager wants to know what you've completed in that weeks' timeframe.

When it comes time to negotiate a raise or land that next job, these are the things that'll come in handy. Plus, they make for great bragging rights!

Experiment with different techniques

As with anything in life, what works for one person might not work for another. When it comes to time management, this is especially true.

Don't be afraid to experiment with different techniques until you find something that works well for you. This could mean trying out a new to-do list format, scheduling software, or even taking breaks at different times throughout the day.

The key is to find what works and stick with it!

Final thoughts

As a Recruiter, it's important to manage your time well so that you can stay productive and avoid burnout. By following the best practices for time management outlined in this chapter, you'll be able to keep your head above water and continue sourcing top talent.

Chapter 15: How to Phone Screen Candidates

Eventually, it will be time to communicate directly with your job applicants via phone.

Phone screenings are a standard part of the process, though they still require a fair amount of preparation beforehand to ensure they go well. When done correctly, they'll help make the next few steps in the recruitment process much easier and reduce wasted time.

What is a phone screening?

As the name suggests, a phone screening is when a Recruiter or hiring manager speaks with an applicant over the phone to determine if they are qualified for a job. This is usually done as the first step in the recruiting process, before scheduling an in-person interview.

Why screen applicants over the phone?

- ✓ It's an easy and cost-effective way to evaluate candidates.
- ✓ You can get a sense of their qualifications and communication skills.

- ✓ It can help weed out unqualified candidates early on.
- ✓ It's a convenient way to assess candidates who live far away.

Ultimately, the main goal here is to determine if the applicant is a good fit for the position and gauge their interest in the role before moving them to the next part of the process.

How to phone screen a candidate

Now that you know what a phone screening is and why you should do it, let's review how to go about conducting one.

The following tips will help make the process smoother and ensure you get the most out of your conversations with potential candidates:

Prepare ahead of time

Like any good interview, you'll want to prepare for your phone screen by doing some research on the candidate. This includes reviewing their resume and cover letter, as well as any online profiles they may have (LinkedIn, Twitter, etc.). It's also a good idea to have a list of questions prepared so you can get a better sense of their qualifications and experience.

Make a good first impression

Remember: This is also your opportunity to represent the company searching for candidates. Don't forget to remain responsive and enthusiastic throughout, and avoid coming across as disorganized or unprepared.

Gauge the applicant's interest

One of the most important things you'll want to determine during a phone screening is whether the applicant is interested in the position. You can do this by asking a few questions about their qualifications and experience, as well as why they are interested in the company and the role.

Keep it brief

Since you're just doing a preliminary evaluation, aim to keep your phone call under 30 minutes. This will help ensure that you have enough time to ask all your questions and get a good sense of the candidate's qualifications without tiring them (or yourself) out.

Take notes

It's important to take notes during your phone call, especially if you're interested in hiring the candidate. This will help you remember key points about their qualifications and experience, as well as any questions you may have for them later on. Questions to ask during a phone screening

The phone screening is a great opportunity to dig a little deeper and receive in-depth information regarding an applicant. As such, you'll want to outline a few "probe questions" beforehand that'll help you receive more than surface-level answers.

A good rule of thumb is to start them off with "What", "How", "Do you...", or "Are you...". Some examples include:

What led you to pursue a career in (specific industry)?
How many years of experience do you have in (specific field)?
Do you know what (specific company) does?

How would you describe your experience working with (specific software)?
Are you familiar with the position's responsibilities?

Here's my Phone Screening Template:

- Are you actively looking?
- When would be your ideal start date be if offered employment? Do you have any deliverables/deadlines that might impact your start date?
- Are you open to relocate? If open to relocation, what locations specifically?
- Have you applied to current roles at my company in the last 6 months or currently in contact with any other recruiters here?
- Please confirm your highest level of education received and the date this was acquired?
- What are your compensation expectations for a new role (base, stock, bonus, etc.)?
    - Do you or will you in future need immigration support work in the US?
    - If yes, what is your current visa status and how long have you held this status? If yes, do you have a valid EAD (work

permit/authorization) and when does your EAD expire? If in H-1B status, please complete the following:
- How long have you been in H-1B status?
- How much time remains on your current-status?
- Do you have any green card applications pending on your behalf?
- Do you have an approved I-140 petition on your behalf? If so, for what position was it filed?
- Do you have an I-485 Application pending? If so, on what date was it filed?

How to discuss the salary expectations

Alright, now comes the most crucial part: discussing the salary.

At first, this might feel somewhat uncomfortable, but you'll benefit both yourself and your candidate by being upfront and straightforward about the role's compensation. If you beat around the bush for too long, you're more likely to simply waste time if it turns out their expectations don't align with the salary you're working with.

Follow the ABCs of Recruiting:

The ABCs of recruiting stands for "Always Be Closing." This principle emphasizes the importance of being proactive, persistent, and focused on securing the best candidates for open positions in an organization.

Bringing someone through the recruiting process only for them to decline the final offer can be highly detrimental to an organization. It leads to wasted time, effort, and resources spent on identifying, engaging, and evaluating the candidate.

Furthermore, it can delay the hiring process, leaving the position vacant for longer, which can negatively impact productivity and disrupt team dynamics. Additionally, a declined offer may cause the organization to lose out on other potential candidates who were overlooked or who accepted other offers during the time-consuming process.

Lastly, repeated instances of unsuccessful recruiting efforts may damage the organization's employer brand, potentially making it more challenging to attract top talent in the future.

The "Always Be Closing" mindset is important for several reasons:

Competitive advantage: In today's highly competitive job market, recruiters must be proactive in engaging and securing top talent. By always keeping an eye on closing the deal, recruiters can act swiftly and effectively to secure high-quality candidates before competitors do.

Enhanced employer brand: By consistently closing job offers with great candidates, an organization can build a strong reputation as an employer of choice. This, in turn, can attract even more top talent in the future.

Reduced time-to-hire: By focusing on closing job offers quickly and efficiently, recruiters can reduce the overall time it takes to fill open positions. This helps organizations minimize the costs associated with vacancies and improve overall productivity.

Increased retention: By securing the right candidates for each position, organizations are more likely to see higher levels of employee satisfaction, engagement, and retention. This contributes to a more stable and productive workforce.

Improved recruitment process: Adopting an "Always Be Closing" mindset encourages recruiters to constantly refine and improve their processes, ensuring they are using the most effective strategies and tactics to secure the best talent for their organization.

In summary, the ABCs of recruiting, "Always Be Closing," is important because it drives recruiters to be proactive, efficient, and effective in securing top talent for their organizations, which can result in numerous long-term benefits.

How to ask a candidate about their compensation requirements?

When asking a candidate about their compensation requirements, it's important to approach the conversation professionally, respectfully, and tactfully. Here are some tips on how to ask a candidate about their compensation requirements:

Choose the right timing: Typically, you should discuss compensation during the initial screening or early stages of the interview process. This helps ensure that both parties have a mutual understanding of expectations and prevents any potential misunderstandings later on.

Be transparent: Start by providing a brief overview of the compensation range or structure for the position. This helps set the context and gives the candidate a reference point for their expectations. Research your states salary laws before this part.

Ask open-ended questions: Frame your question in an open-ended manner that encourages the candidate to share their thoughts. For example, you could say, "Based on your experience and qualifications, what is your desired compensation range?" or "What are your expectations regarding salary and other benefits for this position?"

Be respectful and understanding: Recognize that discussing compensation can be a sensitive topic for some candidates. Approach the conversation with empathy and respect, and make it clear that you're seeking to understand their expectations in order to find a mutually beneficial agreement.

Encourage flexibility: If you sense that the candidate's expectations may be slightly outside the range your organization can offer, encourage them to consider the entire compensation package, including benefits, growth opportunities, and other non-monetary factors.

Reassure confidentiality: Make sure to reassure the candidate that any information they share regarding their compensation requirements will be treated with confidentiality and only used for the purpose of evaluating the potential job offer.

In what stages of the process should you discuss compensation?

Compensation discussions are a crucial part of the recruitment process, and it's important to approach them strategically. Generally, there are two main stages during which compensation should be discussed:

Initial screening or early stages: During the initial screening process, the recruiter should briefly discuss the candidate's compensation expectations to determine if they align with the organization's budget for the position. This step ensures that both parties are on the same page and prevents potential misunderstandings or disappointments later in the process. If the candidate's expectations significantly deviate from the budget, it's better to identify this early on to avoid wasting time and resources on both sides. If the candidate is inclined after the phone screen interview and is set up for a final round – this is another great time to follow up on your compensation questions.

Offer stage or final discussions: Once the candidate has successfully passed through the interview process and the organization is ready to extend a job offer, a more detailed discussion about compensation should take place. This conversation should cover not only base salary but also any bonuses, benefits, stock options, and other forms of compensation the organization might offer. It's essential to provide a clear and comprehensive picture of the total compensation package, as well as addressing any concerns or questions the candidate may have.

While it's possible that compensation may come up in conversations during other stages of the recruitment process, these two stages are the most appropriate times for in-depth discussions. By addressing compensation early on and again at the offer stage, recruiters can ensure a smoother process and increase the likelihood of the candidate accepting the final offer.

How to preclose a candidate before the offer stages

Preclosing a candidate before the offer stage involves gauging their interest and commitment to the opportunity, setting the stage for a positive outcome when the actual offer is extended. Here are some tips to effectively preclose a candidate:

Build rapport: Establish a strong relationship with the candidate throughout the interview process. Maintain open communication and make them feel valued and respected.

Sell the opportunity: Highlight the benefits of working with your organization, including career growth, company culture, and the potential impact of their role. Share success stories of other employees and emphasize how their skills and experience align with the company's vision and goals.

Sell the benefits: Selling benefits to a candidate is essential because it helps attract and retain top talent by showcasing the advantages of working with your organization. By highlighting benefits such as work-life balance, professional development opportunities, and a positive company culture, you demonstrate the value your organization places on employee well-being and growth. This not only appeals to candidates who are looking for more than just a paycheck but also helps differentiate your company from competitors in the job market.

Address concerns: Identify and address any concerns or objections the candidate may have regarding the role, company, or compensation. Listen carefully, respond empathetically, and provide necessary information to alleviate their concerns.

Gauge interest: Regularly check in with the candidate to assess their level of interest in the opportunity. You can ask questions like, "How do you see yourself fitting in with our team?" or "What excites you most about this role?"

Discuss compensation: As mentioned earlier, touch upon compensation expectations during the early stages of the recruitment process. This will help you understand the candidate's requirements and determine if they align with your organization's budget.

Test for commitment: Ask hypothetical questions that help gauge the candidate's commitment to the role, such as, "If we were to extend an offer that meets your expectations, how likely would you be to accept it?" or "Do you have any reservations about joining our organization?"

Understand competing offers: Inquire about any other offers or opportunities the candidate is considering. This information can help you tailor your offer to be more competitive and appealing.

Set expectations: Clearly communicate the timeline for the recruitment process and when the candidate can expect a final decision. This helps manage expectations and keeps the candidate engaged.

Maintain communication: Stay in touch with the candidate between interviews and during the decision-making process. This can help reinforce their interest in the opportunity and keep your organization top of mind.

Preclosing Template:
Preclosing questions are designed to gauge a candidate's interest, commitment, and fit for a role before extending an official job offer. Here are some preclosing questions to ask a candidate:

1. Based on what you know about the role and our organization, what excites you the most about this opportunity?
2. How do you see yourself fitting into our team and contributing to the company's goals?
3. Are there any concerns or reservations you have about the position or our organization that we can address?
4. If we were to extend an offer that meets your expectations, how likely would you be to accept it?
5. What factors are most important to you when evaluating a job offer, apart from compensation?

6. Are there any other job offers or opportunities you are currently considering? If so, how does our opportunity compare to those?
7. What would be your ideal start date if you were to accept an offer from us?
8. Can you provide any feedback on your experience with our recruitment process so far?
9. Are there any additional questions you have about the role, company culture, or our organization?

Chapter 16: How to Produce a Continuous Talent Pipeline

A Recruiter never truly stops looking for talent, even if the company has temporarily slowed its hiring efforts or stopped them completely for a short time.

During this period, you'll want to focus on developing a talent pipeline. Again, recruiting is all about building relationships, which is why it's a good idea to have some "passive candidates" already in your pocket. So, let's get started creating your own.

Building the talent pipeline

The pipeline begins with a dedicated plan and strategy. You need to know what you're looking for and where to find it before anything else.

Establish a foundation

Start by analyzing your current workforce and identifying any gaps. What skills and experience are currently missing? Do you need more people with engineering skills? Or is there a shortage of marketing experts?

Next, you'll want to review your employer branding and candidate experience, which go together. As we reviewed earlier, candidates should have a positive experience when they interact with your company, whether they're simply applying for a position or speaking to a hiring manager. Furthermore, current employees should also feel supported (though this is more of the HR department's job). You can ask them to speak about their positive experiences to encourage job seekers to learn more about the organization.

Look for passive candidates

Recruiters often make the mistake of only looking at active job seekers, which can limit their talent pool. Instead, try targeting passive candidates — those who are currently employed but open to new opportunities.

You can find passive candidates in several ways:

- Mining your company's ATS or CRM for leads.
- Conducting searches on LinkedIn (and other social media sites) for people who meet your criteria.

- Going to in-person job fairs or seminars.
- Seeking referrals from current employees or people in your network.
- Running Boolean searches using the steps detailed in Chapter 10.
- Staying in touch with potential candidates through social media even if they're not actively looking for a new job.

Create a sourcing tracker document

You'll inevitably find it difficult to keep track of every lead you source, which is where the sourcing tracker document comes into play.

Tools like Airtable, Evernote, or Google sheets will help you track and manage candidates by name, company, and other relevant data points. This will develop a database of talent your pipeline leads into, allowing you to turn to a pre-established pool of candidates for the next job opening you come across.

Keep the pipeline flowing

Building a talent pipeline is an essential part of any Recruiter's job. By taking the time to identify your needs and targeting passive candidates, you'll be well on your way to filling any future openings with the best possible talent — in half the time.

Chapter 17: How to Submit a Slate of Candidates

You've finally completed the hard task of sourcing the best candidate possible, and now it's time to showcase your efforts to your client or hiring manager, depending on whether you're an agency or in-house Recruiter.

Believe it or not, the way you present a candidate can be the deciding factor on whether they're hired, so it's important to know how to make the best impression on their behalf.

What goes into a submission package?

In most cases, you're going to want to present your submission package as if the hiring manager knows nothing about the candidate. This will help both them and you review why they were considered a good fit for the role and fill in any empty spaces of knowledge.

<u>The materials your package should detail include:</u>

Candidate skills

You'll want to point out your candidate's experience and skills relevant to the role, ensuring to show how they can satisfy your client's needs. For instance, if they have a specific talent or area of expertise the hiring manager is looking for, this is the time to highlight it.

This is also a great place to showcase any major achievements or accolades the candidate has received. This could be anything from an award they've won to being promoted multiple times at their previous company.

Why you think the candidate is a good fit

Recruiters are relied on for their opinion on whether a candidate is a good fit or not, so make sure to sell your client on the idea that this is someone they should interview or hire.

In your package, be sure to highlight what first caught your attention about the candidate and why *you* think they would be perfect for the role. Discuss factors such as their potential to fit with company culture, their personality, work ethic, and more.

Application materials

Next, you can't forget about the candidate's resume. Take the opportunity to help them update or polish it (with their knowledge, of course) to ensure it's the best representation of their skills and experience.

You should also include a portfolio (if they have one), or any other supplementary materials the candidate may have provided you (testimonials, letters of recommendation, a cover letter, etc.)

A follow up e-mail

Lastly, don't forget to send a follow up e-mail thanking your client or hiring manager for their time and reiterating why you think the candidate is perfect for the role. You can also provide more information if needed and, if all goes well, set up an interview with your candidate.

Additionally, this helps to make sure your package didn't end up lost inside a spam folder!

One step closer to the finish line

Submitting candidates can be a daunting task, but if you follow these guidelines, you're sure to make the best possible impression. By highlighting your candidate's skills and experience, as well as explaining why they're a good fit for the role, you can increase their chances of being hired. As always, don't forget to send a follow up e-mail thanking your client or hiring manager! Finally, after the final round interviews come the offer negotiations.

What are the core principles of offer negotiations?

Offer negotiations are an essential part of the recruitment process, aiming to reach a mutually beneficial agreement between the candidate and the organization. The core principles of offer negotiations include:

- Actively listen to understand motivators
- Aim for a win-win situation
- Indefinitely the real issues up front
- Encourage, restate, and clarify
- Approach the other side with empathy
- Ask open-ended questions
- Know when to walk away
- Don't over communicate -pause and allow the candidate to respond back

- Discuss deadlines and see if they have any other offers in hand

Tips when presenting the offer

Presenting a job offer effectively is crucial for encouraging the candidate to accept and close the deal. Here are some tips for presenting the offer to increase the likelihood of the candidate's acceptance:

Build anticipation: Before presenting the offer, reiterate the candidate's strong performance during the interview process and convey excitement about the prospect of them joining the team.

Personalize the offer: Tailor the offer presentation to the candidate's priorities, emphasizing aspects of the role and company that align with their career goals, interests, and values.

Be clear and comprehensive: Clearly outline the details of the offer, including salary, benefits, bonuses, stock options, vacation time, and any other relevant components. Provide a written summary of the offer for the candidate to review.

Highlight growth opportunities: Emphasize the potential for career growth, professional development, and advancement within your organization to appeal to the candidate's long-term aspirations.

Showcase company culture: Reinforce the positive aspects of your company culture, including work-life balance, diversity and inclusion, and employee engagement initiatives, to demonstrate the value your organization places on employee well-being.

Reiterate the role's impact: Remind the candidate of the importance of their role and the potential impact they can have on the organization's success, appealing to their sense of purpose and ambition.

Be prepared to address concerns: Encourage the candidate to ask questions and raise any concerns they might have about the offer. Be ready to address these concerns and provide additional information as needed.

Set a deadline: Provide a reasonable deadline for the candidate to accept or decline the offer, creating a sense of urgency and encouraging them to make a decision. Usually, it's a 48-hour expiration date clause.

Extend the offer over email with a deadline and then follow up in 1-2 days.

Chapter 18: Developing a Great Candidate Experience

As a Recruiter, you might feel as if most of your focus revolves around speaking to hiring managers, overseeing tasks, reviewing materials, and more. This can make it easy to forget about one of the most crucial aspects of the entire process: your candidate.

Even if they're not the ones providing your commission at the end of the day, how much they enjoy the experience will play a large part in your long-term success in the field. In fact, a poor candidate experience can lead to lower-quality hires, tarnish your company's reputation, and even cost you money.

Fortunately, there are many ways you can improve the candidate experience. You'll find that most of these are simple fixes and can even improve your own workflow in the process, so don't overlook them while detailing your recruitment strategy.
What is candidate experience?

Candidate experience, often abbreviated to "CX", is a term used to describe the entirety of the experience a potential employee has when interacting with your company. This ranges from the time they first hear about your opening, all the way until they either accept or decline your offer.

The goal of creating an excellent candidate experience is twofold. First, you want to make sure that candidates have a positive impression of your company and are more likely to refer others. Second, you want to reduce the chances that a great candidate will go elsewhere because of a poor experience.

How to improve candidate experience

Make sure you have a clearly defined process in place.

If candidates don't know what to expect from the hiring process, they're likely to become frustrated. By outlining the steps involved upfront, you can help ensure a smooth journey for everyone involved.

As you can expect, this'll simultaneously help you remain organized and keep track of your most important upcoming tasks.

Write a detailed job description (including the salary)

The more a candidate knows about the role upfront, the less likely they are to feel surprised by certain responsibilities or expectations you tell them about deeper in the recruitment process.

Furthermore, descriptions that contain key information — such as salary range, company culture, and benefits — are more likely to attract job seekers and reduce time-consuming back and forth communication.

Make the application process simple

When it comes to the application process, less is more. If the steps are overcomplicated and difficult to complete, job seekers will assume they'll have a similar experience working at the company and might turn elsewhere.

So, keep your questions short and easy to answer, and only ask for information that's absolutely necessary. Not to mention, this means you can review their qualifications faster!

Get in touch quickly

Potential employees are busy people, and if they don't hear from you for a few days (or worse, weeks), they may move on. Try to get in touch with them as soon as possible after they've applied.

Not only does this show that you're interested in them, but it also lets them know your company respects employee time and is well-organized — all qualities that'll make your role even more attractive.

Maintain consistent communication (Very Important)

An unskilled Recruiter allows their leads to sit in the dark for extended periods, wondering whether they've been skipped or completely forgotten about.

Even if you reach out to a candidate within a few hours of their application being submitted, you'll need to keep up efficient communication. A single, unanswered e-mail can be all it takes for a candidate to lose interest and move on.

Don't forget: Templates are your friend! Not only do they help keep communication streamlined and quick, but they also make it easier to provide a consistent experience no matter who you're talking to.

I recommend continuous communication with candidates who are in your process. Try and give them a weekly update on next steps in the process. Maybe you are waiting on interview feedback – still send a message to the candidate that you are waiting to hear back on next steps. Never ghost them through the process – always over communicate when you can!

Stay organized

When you're juggling dozens of candidates at once, staying organized is essential for avoiding mistakes and providing a smooth experience. Keep track of each applicant's progress throughout the recruitment process by creating a simple spreadsheet or using an Applicant Tracking System (ATS).

This also makes it easy to identify any potential bottlenecks in your process so you can address them before they cause delays.

Be a great interviewer

No matter how closely you follow the other tips, a bad interview experience can sour a candidate's perception of your company. As such, you'll want to brush up on best practices, such as asking open-ended questions, being on-time, and more. Not only will this help you learn more about the applicant once it's time to meet, but it'll also leave them with a positive impression.

So, from the moment a candidate walks through the door, make sure you're paying attention to their needs. If they need coffee or water, make sure it's readily available. If they have a question, answer it promptly and accurately.

Remember: The little things can make a big difference!

Seek feedback and implement improvements

Even if you think you're doing a great job, there's always room for improvement. After each stage of the recruitment process, ask the candidate for their feedback. This'll help you identify any areas that need tweaking and make sure you're continuing to provide an excellent experience.

Show what makes you great

In a competitive job market, it's more important than ever to make a great first impression with potential employees. By following these tips, you can ensure that candidates have a positive experience from start to finish and are more likely to consider your company when they're ready to make their next career move.

Creating a Great Candidate Experience:
- ✓ Arrive on time.
- ✓ Be friendly and smile.
- ✓ Offer restroom breaks, water/coffee/tea, etc.
- ✓ Explain your role and how that fits into the role they are interviewing for.
- ✓ Explain how the interview will be conducted and what type of questions will be asked.
- ✓ Silence is okay, allow them to think through questions.
- ✓ Explain if you will be typing notes on your laptop but you are listening and attempt to make as much eye contact as possible while doing so.
- ✓ Limit any distractions: turn off your phone, instant messenger, and email notifications.
- ✓ Leave time for the candidate to ask questions on the role, team, etc.

Conclusion

In this book, you've learned some of the most powerful tips utilized by previous, present, and future Recruiters to secure a name for themselves in the industry. When starting your job search, it's important to have a firm understanding of these basics to secure your first role in this exciting field.

However, only by putting them into practice yourself will you be able to take your capabilities to the next level and ensure your work is recognized.

So, what are the steps you'll follow to establish a long and prosperous career? Let's review what we went over:

Chapter 1: Using the Enneagram Personality and Strengths Finder Assessment to determine whether your personality and communication skills are a good fit for the profession.

Chapter 2: Learning to set attainable SMART goals for job searching and career development.

Chapter 3: Identifying the core fundamentals of being a Recruiter.

Chapter 4: Understanding the full-cycle process modern Recruiters use to power their talent sourcing efforts.

Chapter 5: Determining the difference between in-house, agency-based, and freelance recruiting — as well as the salary expectations for each.

Chapter 6: Knowing how to set up informational calls with Recruiters to learn more about the career and start getting connected to recruiting roles.

Chapter 7: Utilizing networking best practices to land a Recruiter job opening.

Chapter 8: Preparing for a Recruiter job interview to land an entry-level Recruiter role, even with no experience.

Chapter 9: Ramping up your new recruiting career and finding a mentor to help you with your professional development.

Chapter 10: Knowing what goes into a recruitment intake meeting to develop a successful partnership with your hiring manager.

Chapter 11: Sourcing talent 101 and the advantages provided by ATS/CRM systems and Boolean strings.

Chapter 12: Writing job descriptions that attract top talent, all while ensuring to avoid unconscious gender bias and remaining within OFCCP employment guidelines.

Chapter 13: Understanding the roles social media, recruitment marketing, and employment branding play in modern recruiting efforts — and how you can use them to your advantage.

Chapter 14: Managing your time wisely to remain as productive as possible and maintain healthy business relationships.

Chapter 15: Phone screening a candidate and discussing their salary expectations without turning them away.

Chapter 16: Developing a talent pipeline that ensures you have a pre-established candidate pool to fall back on for future job openings.

Chapter 17: Submitting a candidate package to your clients or hiring manager to give the applicant the best chance of getting hired. Then offer negotiation talks begin.

Chapter 18: Fostering a candidate experience that leaves candidates with a positive impression of your company, even if they aren't ultimately chosen for the role.

Now that you understand these recruiting fundamental basics, you are better prepared to take the next step in your job search.

Recruiting can be a complex process, but with the right tools and knowledge, you can make the most of every opportunity. So, continue to stay informed, stay motivated, and stay ahead of the competition!

Check out my website [WizardSourcer.com] for the latest recruiting news!

I would appreciate it if you could take the time to write an honest review about my book on Amazon so that others can also benefit from this publication.

www.ingramcontent.com/pod-product-compliance
Lightning Source LLC
Chambersburg PA
CBHW071458220526
45472CB00003B/848